NOTES OF SORROW
SONGS OF JOY

A Memoir

Bobby Lauri

The names and other identifying details of some of the characters in this memoir have been changed, and a few of the stories told to me by my godfather have been compressed, keeping the actual spirit of each but avoiding beating a point to death. These and the other stories in this book are told as I remember them.

This book is intended to provide accurate information with regard to the subject matter covered. However, the author and publisher accept no responsibility for inaccuracies or omissions, and the author and publisher specifically disclaim any liability, loss, or risk, whether personal, financial, or otherwise, that is incurred as a consequence, directly or indirectly, from the use and/or application of any of the contents of this book.

ISBN-13: 978-1985334786
ISBN-10: 198533478X

ROBERT LAURI CONTACT INFORMATION
EMAIL: bjhuns@gmail.com
PHONE: (347) 251-4169

Published by FRM Publishing
6801 Brookeshire Dr. Suite 101
West Bloomfield, MI 48322
Website: frmpublishing.com
Email: faye@frmpublishing.com

Printed in the United States

ACKNOWLEDGMENTS

I offer my heartfelt thanks to my wife Jacqueline, for her outstanding patience and support of this book; my son Michael and my daughter Lisa, who contributed valuable input; my grandfather Michael, who truly loved me; my godfather Charlie Cardali, who was there for me in need; Dr. Almas Nazir, who changed my attitude about life; Dr. Allan Beyda, for encouraging me to proceed when I was dispirited; and Edward R. Levenson and his wife Reva Spiro Luxenberg, for their quality editing. Also, I would like to thank Duncan yo yo for allowing me to use their name in my book being as I became a yo yo champ with their product.

CHAPTER 1

It was midnight and Jacqueline was breathing softly, sleeping peacefully in bed next to me, her arm stretched over mine. I could hardly believe that we'd been married for fifty-five years. Hell, I shoulda been able to shut my eyes and drop off, but I couldn't fall asleep. My mind was churning with thoughts of what had happened to me years ago when we were living in a house in Flushing, Queens and I brought a smile to Frank Sinatra's face when I saw him in Atlantic City.

"Hon," Jacqueline had said then, "Your electric trains are nothing but clutter. Our kids don't want them. We need to throw them out. I heard that Sinatra is a train collector. Maybe he'd like them?"

I had met Frank Sinatra when I was the road manager for the celebrated entertainer Sam Butera. "Road manager" means I was his man Friday taking care of many things. We were in Atlantic City and I waited backstage for Sinatra. When he was ready to go on, my knees shook as I said, "Mr. S. are you into trains?"

Sinatra opened his baby blue eyes wide. "Yes, I am."

I bit down on my lips. "You know, I'm Sam Butera's road manager."

Sinatra straightened his tux. "Yes, I see you with him all the time."

"I have these post-World War II train sets. If you're interested in them, they're yours."

He grinned. "I'll pay you for them."

"Naw. They're a gift from me and if you give me money, they won't be a gift no more." *Maybe I shouldn't of said this next, but I didn't.* "Besides, I'd probably lose the money at the crap table."

This scene, needless to say, was a very pleasant memory, and after I imagined it, I fell fast asleep.

GIFTING FRANK SINATRA MY ANTIQUE TRAINS

Knowing Sinatra and many other celebrities was the good part of my life, but the beginning was really bad. I was eighteen when I first learned about the awful things that had happened to me right after I was born. Since I was close with my godfather Charlie, I turned to him for the whole story. My parents and sisters knew the truth but all those years they had kept it from me.

It was a sweaty day in Corona when I, a cocky teenager of eighteen, stepped through the door of what I called the dress shop. It was really a manufacturing place where many girls worked their fingers to the bone sewing skirts. My godfather cleaned the store and slept upstairs in one little room among three rooms and a small apartment.

I remembered the time when I was thirteen and wanted to work. My godfather had taken me to the basement where there were cutters and steamers. He had said, "Here's the cutter. Follow the pattern." I was so nervous I nicked my finger.

I had yelled, "That's it for me. My cutting days are over."

Now I had the guts to ask my godfather to tell me the truth, the whole truth. I was ready to listen to whatever he had to tell. My godfather sat on his bed with its soiled linen. I sat on a wooden chair that had unsteady legs. The smell of beer was in the air. My godfather drank Schaefer by the quart. A mosquito buzzed around my ear. I swatted it with my hand and it landed on my cheek before it fell to the worn wooden floor "I want to question you about why I was in a home when I was little."

My godfather's expression became serious, and then he started to wave his hands the way many Italians do. "Okay. Here goes. Your momma was in labor for three days. Right after you were born, the nurse in St. John's Hospital watched as your momma—Louise—tried to throw you out the window. She called in the doctor and he said she had a nervous breakdown. She landed in Creedmoor; ya know where the mentally ill people are."

I gritted my teeth.

My godfather continued, "Your two sisters, who were many years older than you, went to two aunts, but no one wanted a crying baby. I brought you to the Angel Guardian Home in Brooklyn. You got sent afterwards to live with a Mrs. Jones. I had $7 in my pocket and couldn't give that woman anything. Your father brought over food. After a while—I don't remember how long—your mother got better and came home from Creedmoor. You were about two years old and Mrs. Jones was attached to you and didn't want to let you go.

She asked your father, 'Are you sure your wife is capable of raising the baby?' Your father gave in to her and went home without you.

Your momma kept asking for you. One day your father returned to Mrs. Jones and demanded his baby. 'I'll bring him next weekend,' she said and sure enough she did.

I remember that when she came the neighbors were setting up a homecoming party in the backyard for you. The smell of the Italian dishes was great and all the food was prepared. Lights were strung up all over, and Italian music was playing. When Mrs. Jones came into the yard she handed you to your momma. You started to bawl. Your momma's face got red, probably from embarrassment and she gave you back to Mrs. Jones who put you down. You stopped crying and you walked around the yard. All of a sudden you started to move your tiny legs to the beat of the music. Then you started to follow the music and sing the notes perfectly. We were all amazed."

"*Goombah*, this is so hard for me to believe."

"Believe it. It happened. The party went on all night. There was plenty of food, wine, and music. There was delicious Italian desserts—*cannoli, sfogliatelle, confetti* candy, and cream puffs. I remember it well. Friends and neighbors had brought all this along with the espresso that the men drank with *sambuca* and lemon peel while they smoked. It was a happy time with you dancing and singing *la la la* until you put your head on the table and fell asleep."

I can't believe my ears.

"Bobby, when the party was ending and people started to go home, you got up and ran after Mrs. Jones who picked you up. You had only known her as your mother, and now she was leaving. Your momma Louise was crying bitter tears. She must've realized that although she gave birth to you, you had belonged to someone else. I saw your father take you from Mrs. Jones's arms and with that she ran out of the yard. You started to cry again."

There was a lump in my throat as my godfather told me this. My heart beat like a drum. What a way to begin a life.

"*Goombah*, I need time to digest this. I'm leaving now. Thanks for telling me the truth."

One morning, many years later, Jacqueline and me were sitting at our kitchen table. She was drinking a cup of coffee while I was reading *The Star,* the morning paper, when I came across a letter in the classified section that read, "Dear Bobby, I hope that in all these years you are doing well. Mrs. Jones."

In a shaky voice I read the letter to Jacqueline who immediately suggested that I call the paper and see if they would give me Mrs. Jones's address or phone number.

Should I do this? After my godfather had told me about Mrs. Jones, I had asked my mother to tell me more about her. She had snapped, "Mrs. Jones never took good care of you."

I decided to tell my mother about my idea of getting in touch with Mrs. Jones, and my mother got so upset that I never did contact her. She had cared for me during my first two years on this earth, and to this day I regret that I never got to speak with her.

I understand my mother's sadness about not being able to care for me from birth. I feel so sorry for her. She not only suffered the loss of her baby for two years but she was completely deaf.

It was a warm summer night, under a full moon, when my mother and me were alone in the backyard. My mother sat on a wicker rocker and I was opposite her on a chair. I touched her arm to make her look at me. She could read lips and I wanted her to answer my question.

"Ma, what happened when you couldn't hear anymore?"

My mother stopped rocking. She used to speak slowly and clearly. "It was eight years before you were born when Susan was a baby. I had a lot of colds and the doctor said my adenoids that sit behind the nose were infected and I needed to have them removed. I had to go to the hospital and have surgery. I was given anesthesia and when I woke up I couldn't hear a sound. The butcher of a surgeon accidentally severed my auditory nerve."

My mother started to rock faster and faster. I could see she was upset. "Ma, you don't have to tell me more."

"I want to. I awoke from the operation stone deaf. Gradually I learned to read lips well, because I had been grounded in language before."

I felt sorry for my poor mother. The shock of that loss changed her life for the worse. I was so angry about the botched-up job on my mother.

AUNT FRANCIS, GODFATHER CHARLIE AND ME BEFORE BEING TAKEN TO THE ORPHANAGE.

CHAPTER 2

I think Patsy wanted me dead. I never called him Pa, Pop or Dad. In my mind he was just Patsy. He didn't deserve my respect. Why did he hate me? That's the mystery of my early life. I can only guess that he blamed me for my mother's post-partum psychosis. Maybe he even blamed me for my mother's deafness, although it happened before I was born. I wish I could ask Patsy, "Why did you make me the outcast of the family."

At the age of six I started going to Catholic elementary school. Back then, kids walked to and from school together without their parents. I came home from school at 3 p.m., but I had no key to get in the house.

I banged on the door with my feet and fists for fifteen minutes to let my mother become aware that I was home from school. She was stone deaf but she could feel the vibration from the banging. There was no one else home at that time since my two sisters were in high school and came home later. Sometimes my mother would be napping and I became worn out with pain in my hands and feet from banging on the door. If my grandfather hadn't owned the apartment house, the rest of the tenants would have complained about that racket every afternoon and we would've been evicted from the apartment. Another mother might have watched the clock to know when I'd be coming home. My mother just wasn't that aware.

When I was seven, my father brought home a set of boxing gloves. I was excited and imagined they were a present for me. Boy was I wrong. My sister watched as he put one glove on me and another one on himself. He started dancing around the kitchen room, jabbing his gloved hand at me. I didn't know what to make of this.

He said, "Come on; let's see how tough you really are." He was my father and I didn't want to hit him so I stood back. If I'd known then that it might be my only opportunity to pay him back for just a fraction of the violence I suffered almost every day at his hands, I wouldn't have hesitated for a second.

My father punched me in the face with a light touch. "Come on, hit me!"

I started to cry, but he kept punching me in the face. I got real mad and hit him as hard as I could. As a result, he punched me so hard that I landed six feet away. That was the end of my boxing lesson.

My father never showed me one ounce of love. He never played catch with me or took me to a ball game. I always wondered if I would survive each day without a beating, or would my sister Nancy snitch on me with the resulting beating from my father. Every day I wondered if I would sleep in my own bed.

So many times I remember staying at my married sister Nancy's apartment until she asked me to leave because she and her husband George were going to sleep. Patsy would've gone into a rage if he learned that Nancy allowed me to sleep over. The spitting mad look on his face scared the hell out of my whole family.

Every time Patsy came at me with the strap I tried to take refuge between the sink and the toilet where there wasn't enough room for him to land the blows. Sometimes my mother did pull him off me.

Today much of what I suffered at my father's hands would be recognized as child abuse. But back then it was not considered abnormal and it was nobody else's place to interfere in the way some parents chose to discipline their children. While the neighbors rarely said a word to my parents, and there were no agencies to call, some did go out of their way to help what they knew I experienced at home, like the neighbor who intervened by getting my broken foot fixed.

Also, when I was seven years old I was playing ball in the park. "Ouch," I cried. I was in terrible pain after one of the neighborhood kids dropped a cinderblock on my foot.

When I limped home neither my sisters nor my father and mother said anything about my limping for two months. One day one of the caring neighbors spoke to my sister Susan.

"Your brother's been limping around the streets for weeks now. I think his foot's probably broken."

Sure enough, when they finally brought me to the hospital for an x-ray, that's just what it was, a broken foot. I had to have a cast put on it. I'm lucky it hadn't healed badly on its own after two months, but I don't recall anyone at the hospital mentioning that. I do remember afterwards that when I needed shoes, Patsy just let me walk around the neighborhood with the sole of my broken shoe flapping at the front, keeping me from walking properly even after my foot had healed.

I lived outside the house from 7 a.m. until dark. I figured out how to unlock the apartment door and run out to find my friends. My sister Susan used to tell my mother to lock the chain on the door so I wouldn't be able to escape. She was the only one who really worried about me. Still, I was a crafty kid. I would wait until my mother was reading the newspaper by the window far from the door. Since she was totally deaf, she wasn't able to hear me leave. I figured out how to put the kitchen chair against the door and stand on it to open the chain lock which was very high up. I then ran out to meet my friends.

When Susan came home she asked my mother, "Why did you let Bobby out?"

"I did nothing of the kind. He must've let himself out."

I was eight years old when I made my First Holy Communion. My classmates' parents were there, standing along the sidewalk leading up to the church, all dressed up in suits and ties. As I walked toward the church with my hands piously folded, my eyes scanned back and forth looking among the parents to see if my father was there. Suddenly, I saw him. He was the only one wearing a tee shirt, work pants, and a kitchen cloth slung over his shoulder. I saw him for a few seconds and then he was gone. I guess my mother had begged him to show up on the street corner to see me, but I wished she hadn't.

In those days kids were regular runners for their parents, doing all kinds of errands all over the neighborhood. My mother used to send me to the butcher to buy some soup bones. The butcher behind the counter gave me the bones with meat on them and marrow in the center.

I used to love to eat the meat and the marrow. When my mother wasn't looking, I would take the soup bone out of the pot and suck the tasty marrow out of the center. *My, it is* delicious*! But, what am I going to do with the bone after I'm finished with it?*

I got scared and put the bone back in the pot. Every time my mother made the soup I did the same thing. One day my father told my mother, "Next time you go to the butcher make sure that bastard gives you bones with marrow in them!"

The following week, when my mother made soup again, I tried to take the bone out of the pot, but she had gotten wise to me and caught me in the act. "It's you who's been eating the meat and marrow off the bones, isn't it?" she sternly asked me.

I nodded, looking at my shoes.

"If your father finds out what you've been doing, he'll take the strap to you!"

From that day on all the bones stayed in the soup pot.

Around this time my friends and I learned to do handstands. While we practiced, we competed to see who could stay on their hands the longest. It was a lot of fun. Some days I stayed up the longest and other days other guys did. One of these contests ended just before we went home for dinner.

When I walked into the kitchen, I saw that my mother was cooking chuck steak in a frying pan on the stove. Anyone who knows anything about meat knows that some cuts of chuck steak are like shoe leather. In order to make the chuck edible, you need to cook it slowly for about four or five hours to soften the fibers.

All of a sudden I got the urge to do a handstand in the kitchen. I did but when I came down from it, my foot hit the handle of the frying pan and sent the pan flying across the kitchen. Chuck steak and gravy plastered the walls, table, and floor. My father was reading the paper in the dining room and he heard my mother screaming in the kitchen.

"Louise, what the hell happened!?" he bellowed.

My mother came into the dining room. "Your son tried to do a handstand in the kitchen. Look what he did!"

My father walked into the kitchen to see, then came out of that messy kitchen screaming, "Bobby!"

Fearing for my life, I ran down the stairs and out to the street. I didn't come home for hours until I hoped tempers had cooled down. My poor mother had some mess to clean up, but I knew that if my father had grabbed me, I would have become as fried as that chuck steak.

That evening—I don't know for sure because I was out in the street—my mother must have made *pasta peseta* (peas and macaroni), a peasant food like *pasta fagiolo* (pasta with beans), which is also considered a peasant food, but tastes better. As far as I'm concerned, I've preferred both meals to chuck steak ever since.

CHAPTER 3

My friends and me used to play basketball in a little park on Corona Avenue next to the Health Department. We chose up sides trying to get the best players for each team. There was this one kid, Jimmy Valvano, who was no more than seven or eight years old and stood about four feet tall, but was a great basketball player. If Jimmy wasn't on my team, I stopped him from shooting the ball by grabbing him around the waist. That drove Jimmy nuts.

He used to yell at me, "Bobby, that's not fair!" and we all got a big laugh.

This kid had a one-handed push-up when he got to the basket, and most of the time the ball went in. I think he had visions of becoming a pro when he got older.

Jim Valvano did go on to become a famous college basketball coach. During his illustrious career, he coached basketball at various colleges, eventually at the highly regarded team at North Carolina State University. Under his guidance, NCSU, in 1983, won the NCAA (National Collegiate Athletic Association) Basketball Championship. If you look at old video clips of those games, he's the excited guy constantly running up and down the court. Sadly, Jim passed away in 1993 from cancer. The V [for "Valvano," of course] Foundation for Cancer Research, which he started shortly before his death, does wonders raising money to fight his type of cancer. His wife Pam is still on the foundation's board of directors.

Just like in the big leagues we played whatever sport was in season: baseball in the summer, football in the fall, and hockey in the winter. I played every sport because it kept my mind off going home to my house of torment. Besides team sports we played other street games too: stick ball, stoop ball, marbles, and hide-and-seek.

We also played "Kick the Can," a kind of a cross between hide-and-seek and tag (and we could play it in teams if we wished). We put an empty can in the middle of the street. One kid would be "it." While "it" counted to twenty-five, everyone else would find a hiding place behind trees and bushes or cars and then the kid who was "it" went looking for another kid. When he found him, he'd tap him on the shoulder, and he'd be sent to the "pen." Someone would try to run over and kick the can without "it" tagging him. If he succeeded, then all the guys holed up in the "pen" would go free and hide all over again. The last one caught became the new "it." This went on and on until we got tired and the game ended.

During those joyful hours at the park with my friends we played another great game called "Buck-Buck." It was a popular street game at that time, and in other neighborhoods it was called "Frog" or "Johnny on a Pony." You needed about ten kids to play. Kids stood in line on one side of the street against a brick wall. Four or five other kids were on the other side of the street, bent over in a line of their own with arms around the waists of the ones in front of them, except, of course, for the first one.

The first kid across the street ran over to "the caterpillar" and jumped on its back. Then, the other kids followed in turn. The object was for "the caterpillar" to hold all the kids up without collapsing. When he finally caved, the game started all over. The best part of the game was the cave-ins, with all of us winding up in a heap, laughing our heads off. As I look back, I doubt if any of us who later might have gotten a "bad back" would think that that game was so funny.

We played with dice for pennies, big stakes for us then. We put equal amounts of our pennies in a pot, then threw the dice against a brick wall and bet. Each player received the amount of pennies according to the roll of the dice. We enjoyed the game so much and played so often that eventually those two dice got worn down to round marbles.

My friends were like family and the street was my happy home. I felt wanted by my friends and wanted was something I never felt at home. When I visited my friends' houses, I was struck by the love I felt there, how differently their parents treated them and their brothers and sisters than the way I was treated by my parents. My best friends at the time were Richie Fernacola and Johnny Piccarella. When we were about ten years old, Richie's mother, whose name was Concetta—Connie in English—could barely speak a word of English and she yelled at Richie in Italian. But even with the high volume you could hear the love in her voice. She made sure he ate well and had the proper clothes for each season. Richie's family loved him and cared about him. I felt cheated out of the love I should've had.

Johnny's parents were stern, but as with Richie's mother, their sternness involved love. Those friends are long gone from my life. Richie, in fact, has, regrettably died; but thoughts of them and the love of their families bring back to me my own crushing memories of fear and neglect.

For a while I moved from group to group and block to block in my neighborhood. Each one-block area had its own group of about six or seven kids who hung out together, and I bounced around everywhere. I never really trusted anyone, even Richie and Johnny, and I never got too close to any of the kids on those blocks, although they were all close friends with each other. For years I couldn't understand why I moved around that way. It took a long time for me to realize that it was because of my family. If you couldn't trust your mother or father, who else could you trust?

People say, "You gotta laugh or you'll cry." So, I guess it's kind of funny to remember how my friends and I were called in from playing by our parents at dinnertime. Richie was greeted at the door with a hug from his mother. Johnny got his hair mussed by his father. Me, I was greeted with a slap on the head from Patsy. Then, I'd sit down with the unsmiling strangers I called my "family" to share our evening meal.

It usually began with my sister Nancy reporting to my father about what she'd seen and heard around the neighborhood that day, including whatever I'd been up to and the scrapes I never could seem to avoid. Nancy was eight years older than me, and we'd always had our differences. Our father was glad to make us tense. So, at that point he would usually beat the hell out of me and slap me so hard in the face that my cheek would turn red. It wasn't so much about whatever my sister told him; it was just an excuse to use his young son as his punching bag.

I was happy spending time with some of the neighbors in our six-family building. They were like family to me. There was Mary Messina, or "Mrs. Tessie," as I called her.

Mrs. Tessie would call up the hall. "Bobby, come down and eat with me. I have steak today." *Oh boy, we never have steak at my house.*

Once a month on a Sunday Mrs. Tessie took me to Radio City Music Hall to hear singers or see a movie. The first show I saw starred Frankie Laine. He was great. After the show, Mrs. Tessie and me went to a restaurant. She seemed to truly love me, maybe because she had no children of her own. I guess that's why we were very close. I used to call her "my second mother."

Teresa was another neighbor who I liked very much. She used to invite me into her apartment. She kept homemade pizza on the window sill of her bedroom. She tore off a chunk and my eyes lit up. No cheese, just tomato sauce. It was so delicious that to this day that's all I ever eat when I order pizza—just tomato sauce and no cheese.

The Giaimo family also lived in my grandfather's building, and I used to watch *The Comedy Show* on TV with their son Danny. They were a kind and wonderful family, even though Mr. Giaimo got annoyed with Danny and me because we laughed so loud at the clowns' antics.

These neighbors must've had some idea about how my father treated me, for they showed me the kindness that he didn't. All of the tenants in our building on a regular basis must've heard the beating and screaming coming from the Lauri home. Patsy didn't give a damn about the neighbors or what they thought. Once in a while, when someone tried to tell him to lighten up on me, he declared, "If you don't like it here, just move."

In those days people would wait in line for an apartment. When I was older, I came to understand that they had been afraid to speak up for me and I appreciated what some of them did say. With everything I went through it makes me feel better to think back and see that there really were people who showed concern for me.

The daily routine of my father's anger and impatience made me behave worse. Many members of the other families who lived in our apartment building showed me kindness, but I repaid them by robbing them. If I saw money in an open pocketbook, I stole it, like I did from our neighbor, Mrs. Tessie.

I stole the five silver dollars someone gave my parents for their twenty-fifth anniversary, which they'd hidden in a panel built into the bottom of the dining-room table.

I remember one time my friends and I wanted to go to the movies. I went over to my father who was sitting at the kitchen table.

"Please, I need a quarter to go to the movies."

"Get lost," he said in his angry voice.

So, what did I do? I stole valuable plumbing materials from the basement. Patsy was a plumber at that time and he did side jobs in our neighborhood, so he kept brass and copper pipes in the cellar of our building. I took some of them that day and sold them to the scrap metal business in the neighborhood. As I continued to steal and sell the materials, I often received enough money to treat all of my friends to the movies. It would have saved my father many dollars if he'd just given me the quarter that first day and kept me away from crime.

I took bags of brass valves and fittings from the basement workshop and my friends helped me carry the bags to the scrap metal yard.

"I'll weigh them," the man who worked there said. We watched as he put them on a scale. Then he paid me the value of the metal, usually about three or four dollars. I was happy, and so were my friends.

One day as my friends and I were walking home, after receiving our payout at the scrap yard, I noticed that they left in a hurry. What I hadn't noticed was that my father was angrily walking toward us. This was because the scrap yard man had finally put two and two together and had called my father on the phone.

"Patsy," he'd said, "your kid was just here with some of your plumbing supplies from your shop and I gave him money for them, but I want you to come and take back brand new valves and brass fittings. I shouldn't have taken them, and I know they belong to you, so send your kid back to get them."

The moment Patsy reached me on the street he started beating the hell out of me. He grabbed me by my hair and didn't let go all the way back to the scrap metal yard.

"Give back the dough," my father screamed. I reached in my pocket and gave it back. "Now carry home the bags of plumbing supplies you stole." I bent over the heavy load and dumped it back in the cellar.

Out came the strap and the beatings began again, along with Patsy's regular insults. "You stupid son-of-a bitch, you'll never amount to nothing!"

Every time Patsy came at me with the strap I tried to take refuge between the sink and the toilet where there wasn't enough room for him to land the blows. When my mother at times did come and pull him off me, I was grateful to her.

One night when I was eight Patsy locked me out of our apartment. I slept on the hallway floor in front of an apartment on the right side. Hours later my mother opened the door while my father was asleep and let me in. I took off my shoes and in my socks, I sneaked down the hall and into my own bed.

After that happened I realized that I wasn't being treated the same way as my sisters were. Whenever I tried to hug my mother, she pushed me away, saying, "Get away, get away!"

Her three days of difficult labor with me, her post-partum psychosis after my birth, and the two years away from her destroyed the bonding that a mother and child need. My father was no better; he also pushed me away any time I tried to get close to him. I came to understand many years later that he blamed me for my mother's breakdown. I had been a change-of-life baby, an accident at that, born eleven years after my two sisters and that made all the difference. I guess Patsy's anger with me was probably due to the circumstances of my birth. Although I was like a virtual stranger in the family, I *was* there and I had to make the best of it.

When I was eleven years old, I was riding my bike on the sidewalk when I passed a parked car that stuck out of a driveway. It blocked my path and I had to suddenly veer into the street. Just at that instant a car hit me as I couldn't get out of the way fast enough, and I was thrown about twenty feet down the street. I was in shock. I jumped up, left my bike, and ran home like a scared rabbit. I was dead set against telling my father since he was against my having a bike. I had managed to have one by salvaging pieces of broken bikes that I found from around the neighborhood and putting them together.

At night someone knocked on the door of our apartment. My father knew the man from the neighborhood. "Come in," he said. My father led him to our living room and seated him in a wine-colored velvet arm chair. My mother and I peeked in at the door.

When I saw that it was the man who hit me, my knees started to shake. *What will Patsy do to me?*

The man's face was white. "Patsy," he said mumbling, "I'm so sorry. I hit your son with my car today. He came out of a driveway into the street as he rode his bike."

I knew I was done for.

The man wiped the sweat off his forehead. "I stopped the car to see if I could help your son, but in a split second he ran away. I was in shock. I knew it was your boy I hit, and I'm here to see if I can be of any help."

My father got up from the sofa. "Thank you for coming, but Bobby is okay. Don't give him a second thought."

After the man left, my father grabbed my hand and pulled me to the backyard. He whipped out his belt and lashed my body until there wasn't a mark on me that wasn't black or blue. He kept saying as he beat me without mercy, "You'll never ride that bike again. You'll never amount to a hill of beans. You hear me?" *I couldn't answer or he'd know he hurt me real bad. I couldn't tell him to stop or it would get worse. He didn't ask me how I felt from the accident or how I got the bike. All I knew was that I hated him with a passion.*

I once made the mistake of asking him for a nickel for the candy store. He glared at me. "You ain't gettin' a penny'," he said. *Instead of him giving me a nickel, I got slapped for asking.*

* * *

One day I playfully swatted my sister Susan with a broom just as my father came out of his bedroom and saw what I did. He went back for a five-pound lump hammer which is a block of steel attached to a handle. I ran for my life down the stairs as the hammer landed next to my foot. I raced out of the house and down the street just in case my father would throw it again and not miss. It would've hurt me terribly and it could of killed me.

Was he unconsciously trying to *kill me and get me out of his life?*

CHAPTER 4

I was eleven when Patsy looked down his nose at me and yelled, "You're old enough to help squeeze the wine grapes." I had to do it because when Patsy told me to do something, I trembled and obeyed. The grapes were from the Four Brothers store down the block. In the fall everyone bought grapes from them and squeezed them to make homemade wine. The Four Brothers got their grapes from the wholesale depot for retail sales in their store. I used to watch them unload as I spent plenty of time in the street trying to avoid my father's beatings. The average customer bought about eighteen boxes to make a fifty-five gallon barrel of wine. But Patsy and my godfather bought as much as a truckload to make sixteen barrels.

I squeezed the grapes for half a week in the damp dark cellar lit by low wattage bulbs. It was just the three of us in the cellar, my godfather Charlie, Patsy, and me. We used three kinds of grapes and took turns cranking the grinder. The grape juice landed in a bucket. I had to lift the bucket when it was full and pour it into a fifty-five gallon oak barrel. We filled sixteen barrels.

The smell was horrible. It could make a person drunk. I tottered around and kept squeezing. Patsy used to say, "Keep goin'. Don't stop. We need the wine."

Over and over I turned the handle on the box that had teeth in the grinder. Every grape that I squeezed so much felt like I squeezed the life out of them. After a week the grapes fermented and dark red wine was produced. The toughest part was carrying the boxes up the staircase out of the cellar. It was back breaking for an eleven year-old kid.

But my work, for which I never got a nickel, wasn't done. I helped load the waste skin and vines into the empty boxes. Then I hauled the boxes into the backyard. Is it a wonder I fell asleep in class?

* * *

One morning when I was throwing my ball against the brick wall in the backyard of my godfather's house, I noticed two men, one short and one tall who were wearing suits, approach the front gate. They walked towards me in the backyard, and I had no idea what they wanted.

The short one said, "This is the place."

The other one asked me, "Hey kid, where's the owner of this building?"

"He's in the house. Wait a minute. I'll get him."

I ran to call my godfather Charlie. "*Goombah*, there are two men in the yard who want to talk to you."

"I'll take care of it," he said.

I heard the tall man say to my godfather, "You're running a still." In fact, the smell of two hundred boxes of squeezed grapes was all over the whole yard.

The government guys asked my godfather Charlie to open the basement door. They went down the steps and counted sixteen barrels of wine.

The taller of the two said, "Only two barrels of wine are allowed per person!"

Charlie answered, "You're correct! Two are for my neighbor, two for my brother, and two for a friend."

The man said, "That makes only six."

My godfather then came up with five more people.

"Okay, wise guy," one man said. They left in a huff.

Later my godfather found out that a man in the neighborhood had ratted on him and Patsy about the number of the wine barrels in the cellar. The informer was a person they had refused to sell wine as $5 was the cost and the man wouldn't pay their price. Their business was good for their neighbors, but they nearly got slapped with a criminal charge.

CHAPTER 5

My grandfather Michael stayed at home with us on Sundays instead of playing cards with his friends, because every Sunday, as I said, we had a big family dinner. My mother made meatballs with gravy, sausage, and *brasciole*, which is beef flank sliced very thin. She laid out the slices on the kitchen table, then stuffed each one with Italian cheese, parsley, garlic, salt, and pepper, rolled it up and tied it with some heavy string. Sometimes she held it together with toothpicks. When the *brasciole* slices were cooked and you took them out of the pot of gravy, you had to struggle to remove the string, but the feast was so delicious that it was worth it.

During the meal arguments flew back and forth across the dinner table between my grandfather at one end of the table and Patsy at the other end. The dinner started out fine, with glasses of homemade wine poured for all the adults. But after drinking a few glasses of that homemade wine my father started in on me. After I'd been slapped over and over for many nights for every little thing my sister reported, I suddenly thought of a plan to escape the reaches of my father's hand.

I asked my godfather to switch seats with me, and from that point on, I was out of my father's range.

Patsy always wanted to control us, poison my relationships with my sisters, and create hate and violence. In the last two matters he almost succeeded. The more he tried to control me the more rebellious I became and the more trouble I got into. I became what I was taught. It seemed that the only way I knew how to live was to get into trouble.

* * *

When I was in Catholic elementary school, I misbehaved so much that my first-grade teacher kept me back and I had to repeat the year. The same thing happened in the sixth grade, making me that much older than the other kids.

Most of the teachers at school were nuns, but their religion didn't stop them from slapping. Most of my classmates were shocked when they got slapped in the face, but not me. I was used to that treatment.

There was one lay teacher in the school, Mrs. Karp, who taught the fifth grade. She was always very well-dressed. Her nails were always manicured and she wore jewelry every day. But she beat kids to a pulp.

One day a good friend of mine was late to class and Mrs. Karp gave him a stern look. He started to laugh, and Mrs. Karp went out of her mind. She picked up the window pole that was used to open the windows. It had a small knob which fit into a hole on top. She broke the pole over his back. Can you imagine the force she applied when the pole split in two? She would be fired for that today, but in those days they called it discipline.

Some discipline! It made my classmates and me so angry that we did whatever we had to do to get revenge. We did anything we could think of to be nuisances in class. We threw erasers and chalk out the windows. My friend loosened coatroom hooks before class, causing coats to fall on the floor. My friends and me never snitched on one another. If the teacher asked you to tell her who did something, you said nothing; you took a punishment for that and kept your mouth shut. This was fair, because we all eventually had our turns at rough treatment.

As punishment for the major misbehaviors we had to write whatever the wrongdoing was five hundred times, for example, "I will not act up in class," or "I will not loosen up the hooks in the coat room." Or, we spent two hours in the convent sitting in a chair and doing nothing until the sister there would say, "Master Lauri, you may go home." For me, to be sure, the punishment at home was always worse than the punishment at school.

One day my buddy Mikey Pennachio and me wanted to see a movie down in Corona Village, which was the downtown area of the Corona section of Queens. The movie was to start at one in the afternoon. Our school lunch hour was between noon and 1:00 p.m., so I came up with a plan to get to the theater on time. In those days a movie ticket included two feature films and short comedies.

In the schoolyard at recess I had noticed a pencil sharpener sitting on the windowsill. It was early in September and the weather was still hot and summery, so all of the school's windows were thrown open to catch any hint of a breeze.

I let Mikey in on my plan, which was to steal the pencil sharpener from the windowsill. We went to the movies and returned to school just as class was letting out for the day. Sister Superior, who was the principal of our school, said, "Where have you been all afternoon?"

I spoke up. "We seen some kid steal the pencil sharpener and run away. We chased him in and out of every block. When we finally cornered him, we had to fight him to make him give back the pencil sharpener."

Sister Superior smiled broadly. "I'm proud of you boys."

I couldn't believe my ears. My plan worked like a charm and we were suddenly heroes instead of truants. We had received a pat on the head instead of a slap in the face.

My seventh-grade teacher was Sister Catherine, a nun who was no match for me and my friend Mikey. We played every trick on her in the book. Mikey and me stole chalkboard erasers when she wasn't looking and threw them out the window. When she got up to write on the board, one of us put gum on her chair. Her habit stuck to the chair after she sat down and tried to get up again. A few of our classmates were angry with what we done, but nobody dared snitch.

One day Sister Catherine announced that we'd be having a contest to see who could bring in the most coupons from the tops of a popular brand of macaroni boxes. A generous gift from the company was to be the prize for the winner. Mikey and me pooled our coupons together figuring that one of us would win the contest and we'd share the prize. But we found that we had a challenger by the name of Frankie Falco, whose mother was the president of the Mother's Club. Frankie was a real mama's boy and we simply couldn't let him win the contest, but his mother was supplying him with hundreds of coupons daily. No matter how hard we tried, Mikey and me couldn't keep up with the amount of coupons Frankie was bringing in, and so we put our heads together and came up with an idea.

We brought in our coupons in a bundle wrapped with a rubber band. Then we put them in an open cabinet covered by a drape cloth. Mikey distracted Sister Catherine by raising his hand with a pretend question, and when Sister Catherine went over to Mikey's desk to help him, quietly I snuck over to the cabinet, moved the drape cloth to the side, and removed as many of Frankie's coupons as my pockets could hold. We did that a couple of times a week.

Sister Catherine kept a daily tally of everyone's coupon totals on the blackboard. Before long Mikey and me had overtaken Frankie for first place, with a healthy lead, from all the coupons we'd collected and the ones we'd stolen from the cabinet.

Our lead didn't last long since Frankie started coming into class every day with a huge bag of coupons. Mikey and me looked at each other, "What do we do now?" The contest was almost over, and we were still sticking to our plan and trying to keep up with the golden boy. Frankie's mother did everything she could to help her son win. Later we learned that she'd collected hundreds of coupons from the Mother's Club. By the end of the contest Mikey and me stole more than a thousand coupons and we still lost to Frankie.

When Mikey and me got bored in class, we each raised our hands to go to the lavatory and we hung out there to relax. There were rolling metal coat racks in the hallway, the kind with four wheels and a six-foot bar across the top. Some of these were extra coat racks from the wintertime that were kept in the hall. In fall and spring these were empty.

A few times Mikey put a coat rack in the middle of the hallway about ten feet from the two swinging doors. I ran down the hallway, jumped onto the empty rack, grabbed the top of the bar, and flew down the remaining distance of the hallway into the swinging doors. That rack hitting the swinging metal doors sounded like a huge explosion. Mikey and me ran back to our classroom laughing hysterically. That kind of fun and laughter never happened at home. I guess I had to find my fun in any place I could.

The hours after school and on weekends were for playing outside and running around with packs of friends, which led to its share of scrapes. I had my share and about three other guys' shares combined. But no matter what happened to me, how hurt I got, or how much pain I was in my father never batted an eye nor shed a tear; he didn't spend a moment of worry.

CHAPTER 6

One spring day my friends and me took a walk to the lemon ice store. "Hey," Richie said, "Look at that. Someone put an old refrigerator on the sidewalk." In those days taking off the door wasn't required. I looked at the refrigerator and saw that it was one of the first refrigerator models, the kind with the compressor on top. Since I had always been a curious kid, I opened the door to the fridge.

The next thing I knew heavy fumes from the compressor's leaking chemicals overcame me. I screamed, and everything went black. I thought I had gone blind. Richie held my hand and led me into Louie's Pork Store. While I stood there blinded and screaming, my friends told Louie what had happened to me. Louie had the good sense to wash out my eyes and the chemicals started to go away. Slowly I began to see again.

My father never noticed that my eyes were red for a week, and by some stroke of luck my sister Nancy either didn't learn what had happened or didn't tell him. He'd have slapped me and called me stupid for opening the refrigerator door.

* * *

One freezing December day my friends and me were hanging out in a vacant lot on 48th Avenue when Mikey said, "It's so darn cold. Let's make a bonfire."

"Yeah, good idea," Richie said, "and we'll put in long steel rods from that broken fence."

I added, "We can make spears and play medieval warriors."

Now the steel rods were about five feet long and one-inch square. We agreed that the spears would become red hot on the ends. That would be dangerous. But one of my friends, I don't remember which one, played a prank on me. He turned "my" rod around so that the hot point was sticking out. I couldn't tell it was hot because it had cooled down to a black color. When I grabbed the rod, my hand stuck to it. I screamed my head off and ran home, rushed straight into the bathroom, and ran cold water over my hand until it felt a little better.

My sister Susan came in and got panicky when she saw how badly my hand had been burned. She thought that putting butter on my hand was the right thing to do; but the pain only got worse, so I ran back to the bathroom to wash the butter off with cold water. The pain was so bad I suffered all night and couldn't sleep a wink. It was at least a second-degree burn and it took weeks to heal. Either Susan didn't tell our parents or they just didn't care. They never said a word about my burned hand.

* * *

I can honestly tell you that all of these things really happened to me, and more. Whether I was right or wrong, Patsy never defended or supported me. He never showed one bit of warm emotion. He was as cold as ice, even when I got shot in the face with a zip gun. I was about ten years old when I went with my parents one afternoon to visit my Aunt Frances who was also my godmother. She lived in a house on Corona Avenue and I soon got bored with the grownups' talk. I didn't announce that I was going to Brown's candy store around the corner.

As I walked into the store, I saw a bunch of older kids from my neighborhood hanging out there. Chappy was one of the guys, and it was well-known that he was a bad dude. All of a sudden he pulled out a gun. I thought it was a cap gun because it didn't look real to me. He started to show all the guys in the candy store the gun, and as I went closer, I saw that it was a zip gun which he had made out of a cap gun. He pointed it right at me laughing, and the gun accidentally went off and its projectile hit me on the bottom of my left cheek. Blood started running down my face. I bawled as I raced out of the store and back up to Aunt Frances' house. When my aunt saw the blood running down my face, she became frantic. My father just sat calmly on the sofa, not the least bit concerned.

Aunt Frances said, "What happened to you?"

Between tears I told her, "Chappy, an older guy, shot me in the face with a gun."

When Patsy heard this he shrugged his shoulders. He couldn't have cared less.

Aunt Frances said as she washed the blood from my face with a washrag, "Bobby, didn't you know that kid is the nut of the neighborhood?"

I kept sniffing.

Aunt Frances said, "I see a lot of pockmarks on your lower left cheek."

When she said that my cousin Ronnie went off to Brown's candy store to find out what had happened. Fifteen minutes later he came back and said, "Bobby was shot by Chappy with a handmade zip gun."

Nobody did anything after that. Patsy didn't go down to the candy store to stand up to Chappy, nor did he call the police. Chappy was never punished. In the following days, as my cheek started to heal, I noticed I couldn't see very well out of my left eye. But, as usual, it was a long time until anyone else took notice.

* * *

Months later, during another afternoon hanging out at Brown's candy store, the guys and me must've been getting too loud for Mr. Brown, so he asked us to leave. As I walked past him, he slapped me in the back of my head. My friends started laughing, but I saw red.

There was some brick work being done on a building across the street from the candy store, so I walked across the street, picked up a brick, and went back to the front of the store. My friends stopped laughing. They just looked at me. I could tell they were wondering what I was going to do with that brick.

I knocked on Mr. Brown's store window, and when he came to see who was knocking and saw me with the brick in my hand, he turned as white as a ghost. I looked right at him with a big smile and threw the brick into the dead center of that five-foot-square glass. I heard him screaming *bastardo.* He called me a bastard in Italian but I didn't care. My friends and me just ran away.

Later that night when I was sleeping, my father heard a knock on the door and, as you would guess, it was a police officer. He told my father what had happened that afternoon at Mr. Brown's. "Your son threw a brick at the candy store window around the corner and the owner wants him arrested."

My father looked at the cop, pointed to my bedroom, and told him, "The son-of-a-bitch is in there."

The police officer opened the bedroom door and tapped me lightly on the shoulder with his nightstick to wake me. As I sleepily opened my eyes, he said, "Sir, you have to come with me."

As I quickly dressed, I heard my father say to the cop, "Keep the son-of-a-bitch locked up!"

He must have been thrilled to have a chance to be rid of me.

This wasn't the first time he had eagerly turned me over to the police. The summer before, I had given a pack of fireworks to some neighborhood kid. When the police caught him setting them off, the kid gave my name to one of them and he came to our house. He told my father what had happened and my father gave me up even faster than it took that kid to give my name.

In those days if the police picked you up as a minor for an offense, you would get a Juvenile Delinquent Card, called a J.D. Card. The court, of course, kept a record of the incident. If you got too many of those cards, you'd be sent to Reform School. In spite of Patsy's wishes the police didn't keep me locked up for throwing the brick through Mr. Brown's window.

The following week a notice came home from one of my teachers at school informing my parents that I couldn't see the writing on the blackboard even after the teacher had moved my desk to the front of the class. My father didn't care and my deaf mother never seemed to know what was happening to me, or to anyone else in the family. She never spoke to us about any family matters; she left that up to my sisters and my father. My oldest sister Susan brought me to Dr. Berg, the eye doctor down in the Village. He gave me an eye test and he found astigmatism in my left eye and he also noticed some damage to the eye from that gunshot wound I'd received almost a year earlier. Nobody mentioned the gunshot to Dr. Berg. He prescribed glasses for me to wear

As Richie, Johnny, and me walked one morning to the area of the "World's Fair" grounds in Flushing Meadows Corona Park to hang out and play hide-and-seek, our route took us by some railroad tracks about two blocks from my house. Richie picked up a railroad spike, a huge nail that the railroad workers used to hammer on the side of a track to hold it in place. Loose spikes were all over the place, on the grass, and on the stones by the track.

Richie said, "If I throw the spike onto the third rail, the juice from the rail will magnetize the spike. We can use it as a magnet."

So Richie and Johnny threw their spikes onto the third rail and nothing happened. When I went to throw my spike, the electrical current in the rail caught the spike. My whole body shook from head to toe, and all the hair on my head stood straight up.

My friends said that they will remember my screaming and the expression on my face for the rest of their lives. There must have been enough voltage in that rail to cause instant death.

If you have ever gotten an electric shock from a wall outlet or a frayed wire, you've felt the shaking of your hand, the strange sensation, and the fear. Now, imagine those feelings from a shock a thousand times more powerful than a wall outlet.

How is it possible that I wasn't killed? First, I wasn't grounded. The electrical current from the rail to my body was weakened by the fact that I was wearing rubber-soled sneakers. Secondly, Richie picked up a board and knocked me away from the rail without my feeling the blow.

The first words out of my mouth were, "Am I still alive?"

Johnny and Richie laughed, and for once I didn't mind being laughed at. Johnny and I never told anyone about it, but Richie told his brothers Tony and Nicky. At first they didn't believe it; but the next day when Tony saw Johnny, he asked Johnny about it and Johnny confirmed it, "Sure enough Bobby caught the third rail's current and lived to talk about it!"

I never told my father or anyone else in my family what happened to me.

RAILROAD SPIKE

One Saturday morning in the summer, my buddies Richie and Johnny and me decided to go camping. We went to the grocery store and bought some potatoes and a couple of cans of pork and beans. At 8:00 a.m. we went to the neighborhood park and found a beautiful place deep in the woods to set up our "tent," a sheet and four sticks in the shape of an A-frame. We started a little fire and put the potatoes in it. We baked them nice and crisp and when they was done, I put them on a metal plate and we went into our tent to eat them.

Richie and Johnny started to eat, but before I did, I said, "I'm going to put the two cans of pork and beans in the fire." After I did that, I went back into the tent to eat my potato. We were having such a great time eating and laughing when all of a sudden we heard an explosion outside of the tent. It was the cans I had put in the fire. They had exploded all over the fire, tent, and surrounding area.

Richie asked, "Did you put little holes in the cans to let the steam out before you put them on the fire?"

"I didn't know that." That day for lunch we only had potatoes.

We walked all through the woods and thought we were real hikers. When it got dark, we started to walk home; and when I got near my house, my sister Susan ran toward me. As soon as I saw the look on her face, I thought, *Boy I'm in trouble!*

Susan said, "Where've you been all day? I thought you were dead somewhere!"

But after she was finished scolding me, she started to hug and kiss me. She was crying from relief. I knew then that she truly loved me, that there was one person in my family who did. Susan was very close to my father and Nancy was close to my mother, and I was the son that wasn't close to nobody. Now, at least, I knew that someone was glad I existed.

CHAPTER 7

I'm not sure why my father even bothered to help me with my homework. He'd sit with me at the kitchen table and take out pocket change. "Here's a nickel and a dime and two pennies. How much do they add up to?"

After I thought for a second and scratched my head I said, "Eighteen cents."

I got a slap to the back of my head. "You're a dunce. You'll never amount to nothing."

If I bought home a report card with an "Unsatisfactory" in Conduct, I knew Patsy would beat me with a strap. If I managed to get a "Satisfactory", which was not often, I'd be spared.

The only person who really comforted me when I was very young was my grandfather Michael, my mother's father. He was the most respected man in the neighborhood. By the time he was thirty-seven years old in 1902 he had already owned and built two six-family houses on Corona Avenue. The people in the neighborhood called him *Stim Michele* (Sir Michael) in Italian.

My grandfather lived with us and, as a boy I shared a bedroom with him. He had the bed, while I slept in the pullout. My parents had the larger bedroom and my sisters shared the bed in the pullout couch in the dining room.

Every morning my grandfather said to me, "Bobby, please wash my feet."

I ran to get the bucket, filled it with warm water, and washed his feet with a soapy cloth. Then after I dried his feet with a towel, he'd say, "Now put on my clean white socks."

I would struggle to get each sock on.

Then he'd say, "Now my shoes."

After this routine my grandfather would nod his head and say, "Good boy. Now Bobby, go to Mr. Brown's candy store and get me *The Progresso* and my cigar."

The Progresso was the Italian daily paper and his Italian cigar looked like a piece of rope. When I came back, I would stand in front of him and he would unsnap his coin purse, pull out a nickel and give it to me. That made me the happiest kid in the world. Then I would meet my two friends Richie and Johnny and we would go to Mr. Brown's and spend the nickel, which, in those years went a long way.

At that time we lived in one of the six-family houses my grandfather had built and owned. He also owned an old dilapidated two-family house across the street. When he bought it a fruit store was on the ground floor, but in time the store closed down.

Every morning, when I was too young to go to school, after breakfast I went with my grandfather to the house across the street. We stayed there all day until it was time to go back home for dinner. We had lunch together and on colder days my grandfather lit the old pot-bellied stove in the kitchen for warmth. On Sundays we ate dinner with the whole family.

Every day besides Sunday my grandfather and some of his neighborhood friends used to play cards in the old house. Four people played an Italian game called "3/7." Whoever won got to drink the beer they kept in a white enamel pail, while the losers watched and complained. Then they'd start another game, and this went on all day long, with the losers getting angry that they'd lost. On top of that the losers would have to watch the winners drink the cold beer, especially on hot summer days. I used to hang around there all day with my grandfather and his friends until we were ready to go back home.

One day as I was playing outside with a pink rubber ball, throwing the ball against the wall of a brick building and catching it with my baseball glove, I heard my grandfather calling me in Italian. I went inside to him and he told me, "Go next door to the Cozy Nook Bar with this can and ask the man to fill it up with beer." He handed me the white pail, which had a cover, and a quarter to buy the beer.

THE BEER PAIL

I quickly threw my ball and glove into another room and ran to the Cozy Nook Bar. I'd been sent there many times before. The bartender filled up the white pail for me and I left to bring the beer back to my grandfather.

When I went to get my ball and glove, I found the glove but I didn't find the ball. The men were still playing cards. I searched all over for the ball but I couldn't find it. I started looking in all the corners of each room, even under the furniture. Then I decided to look under an old bed in a corner of a back room. As I put my hand under the bed I screamed holy murder. You could not imagine that a scream that loud could come from a five-year-old boy. SNAP–my hand had gotten caught in a rat trap. I kept screaming my head off but I couldn't get the trap off my hand. A commotion arose in the other room by the men who wondered what had happened to me.

MY GRANDFATHER AND MY MOTHER.

I raced into the room where they were playing cards with the rat trap hanging from four of my little fingers. My grandfather pulled the trap off my hand. Then he pulled me close and held me, rocking me back and forth. I still remember him wiping the tears from my face. *How could I not love a man like this?* It was so different from my life at home. Comforted, I went back to look for my ball and found it under the bed where it had rolled near the rat trap. I returned to my playing in the yard, throwing the ball against the brick building as if nothing had happened. We never mentioned the incident to my father, not only because he wouldn't have cared, but also because all I would have gotten from him was a beating for being careless with my things. So, without a word spoken between us, my grandfather and me kept this as our secret.

As miserable as my life in the Lauri household was, when at the age of eight, I left that house in the early morning, I found happiness in the streets. Every day there was a new adventure on Corona Avenue and the streets and blocks throughout the neighborhood. You never knew what the day was going to bring. I seldom ate lunch at home. In those days I went to the neighborhood grocery store and for fifty cents got a liverwurst sandwich on hero bread with onion and lots of mustard, and a bottle of soda.

My friends and me enjoyed our lunches together at Spaghetti Park on Corona Avenue. We played cards for matchbook covers, flipped baseball cards, and traded baseball cards and bottle tops for matchbook covers and comic books. Our neighborhood was a few square miles in a large city, the entire world to us.

On hot summer days my buddies and me went to the lemon ice store, and for a nickel we got a large cup of lemon ice. Then, we headed over to Brown's for a famous egg cream made with a little milk and chocolate or vanilla syrup. Mr. Brown put the glass under the fountain dispenser, pulled the handle forward to squirt out seltzer before pushing the handle back. The forceful stream of seltzer made the perfect frothy egg cream. Mr. Brown also made the best malteds, creamy and very cold with milk and ice cream. When he put one under the three-blade spinner, we saw the malt rise to the top of the canister. The first gulp was heaven, and the rest was just as good.

One rare day when I was home at lunchtime I saw that my father was making a sandwich for himself.

"What're you makin'?"

"None of your business."

Two slices of bread were in the toaster. When my father took a package of bacon out of the refrigerator, I thought, *Mmm, nice crispy bacon on toast with lettuce and tomatoes.* At that moment, I started to feel hungry, but then I saw my father take the toast out of the toaster and put raw bacon on it. I couldn't believe that he didn't want to cook the bacon.

I suddenly realized how much fun I could have with this since every time I brought my sandwich to eat at the park with my friends Richie jumped up and asked me for a bite. As soon as my father left the kitchen, I made another sandwich the same way, raw bacon on toast. I wrapped it up and went to the park.

Four or five of the guys were there playing cards for matchbook covers. I could see Richie's eyes light up at the sight of the sandwich in my hand.

"Whatcha got there, Bobby?"

"Oh, just my sandwich."

"Gimme a bite!"

Richie was all over it, so I unwrapped it and handed it to him. He bit off a huge chunk, chewed for a few seconds, and with all the guys watching, spat it out.

"Bobby, what the hell did you bring?!"

"Just a raw bacon sandwich, Rich."

With that my friends started to laugh their heads off. Richie was so mad he threw that sandwich at me and chased me all over the park. That was the best prank of the year.

* * *

From the time I was about ten years old I pretty much supported myself with whatever money I could make. I sold rags, paper, and junk. When my old pants or dungarees got holes, or I outgrew them, I used the money to buy new ones. I don't know where my clothes had come from before then because I don't remember my parents ever buying me any.

I shined shoes on the weekends to make some extra money. I worked for the Four Brothers delivering wine grapes on their truck in the fall, and I worked for Morris Potash, who owned the largest fruit and vegetable store in town. I rode with three or four workers to the wholesale produce market at Hunts Point in the Bronx. We loaded heavy boxes of fruits and vegetables onto the truck and unloaded them when we got back to the store. That took from six in the morning until nine, and I made only $3.00 for the long and tiring morning's work.

Sometimes my father forced me to go on side jobs with him. "I'll kick the stuffing out of you if you don't go with me," he used to say.

If I didn't, I was slave labor because he got paid and kept the money for himself.

Once when we worked at Fisher's Bakery, he tossed me an apple pie at the end of the job.

Again, when we worked in Clapper's clothing store, he got me a tie. He bartered work for his lawyer for free legal advice. I got nothing. From the examples of the apple pie and the tie, though, I can't say that I got "absolutely nothing" from him.

On Monday nights I helped work the bingo games at the church school. The woman in charge of running the bingo night was a woman from the Volunteers' Club. Many other women helped run and call the games. One day the woman in charge called the school with a request.

"Please have Bobby Lauri come to my house and bring new bingo cards for the night session for the school."

When I entered the woman's house, I noticed that it looked just like a picture out of *Good Housekeeping.* She had the most beautiful furniture I had ever seen. I was in awe. I wondered how she and her husband could afford such a rich home. This woman had no job and her husband was a manual laborer earning minimum wage. Where could they have gotten the money for all of those beautiful furnishings? Bingo money, of course!

That night I spoke to my friend Conrad Mateo. "You won't believe that this dame has a house fit for a millionaire. Furniture like what I never saw in my life."

Conrad and me put our heads together and came up with the idea that she must be skimming the bingo pot.

"Let's take a small cut for ourselves," I said knowing absolutely that it was wrong. But to me, it was all right since they fed us boys who helped with the games cheese sandwiches which are treats for mice.

I went through life with a nagging feeling that I was always getting the short end of the stick. It felt like everything important was lacking: love, money, and respect. I worked for my father and earned nothing but insults. Other kids got hugs and I got smacks. I constantly wanted justice.

ME AND MY MOM

CHAPTER 8

I became an altar boy at church when I was eleven years old, figuring that if I turned to God, maybe He would help me change my life and make things better for me. One day while I was serving Mass, I couldn't remember the Latin for the *"Confiteor,"* the prayer you say when you confess your weekly sins to God. We had a tough Irish priest by the name of Father McMann. In those days the Mass was said in Latin and the altar boys' responses were in Latin.

Father McMann was saying the prayers when he looked over and caught me talking to my fellow altar boy.

"Hurry, tell me the Latin we got to say," I whispered.

When the altar boy started to talk Father McMann spoke to both of us in an angry voice. "Get off this altar right now."

The whole congregation watched us as we left with our faces red as beets and looked for a seat. But in those days you couldn't get a seat at Mass if you were late; you had to stand against the wall. I was so embarrassed that I left church that day. I didn't attend church for a year after that and I never served Mass again. I did make peace with the priest, however, and returned to church for my confirmation.

As I have mentioned, my grandfather owned our six-family house on Corona Avenue. It was one of two that he'd built side-by-side in 1902. The apartments were cold-water flats and the rent was $19 a month.

Every month on the first of the month, my mother gave me six $1 dollar bills and told me to go around to the other six tenants and collect the rent. Each one gave me a twenty-dollar bill and I returned a dollar bill back as change.

Maria, a tenant on the second floor used to yell in the hallways and my mother got complaints from other tenants that she had to shut Maria up. No matter what time of the year it was Maria wore a heavy, quilted dress with a handkerchief around her head.

One day I said to my mother, "Maria must have a lot of money in that apartment."

"No," my mother told me, "She's a very poor lady and doesn't have much money at all."

"When I collect the rent every month," I replied, "Maria pays me with an old twenty-dollar bill which is always very flat like it has just come off of a pile of other money." *I really wondered about that.*

As I was walking home from school one afternoon, I saw an ambulance in front of our building. The emergency medical technicians had Maria on a stretcher. They put the stretcher in the ambulance and off they went to the hospital.

We learned later that she'd had a massive heart attack and died.

"Go, Bobby, clean out Maria's apartment," my mother said.

"Okay." But when I got there, my father was already there with a police officer.

"Help me move Maria's mattress," my father ordered.

I helped and I wasn't too surprised when we found a layer of twenty-dollar bills pressed between the mattress and box spring. My eyes lit up. I had known there was money in that apartment.

The police officer counted a total of $8,500.

"Ma," I said later. "Maria hid $8,500 under her mattress. What do you think of that?"

My mother's jaw hung down. "I can't believe it!"

Since Maria had had no known living relatives, all that money went to the state coffers. But I learned then and there that you can never tell a book by its cover!

***

One day I approached Patsy, "Can I use the store across the street for a club for me, Richie, and Johnny?"

"Okay, as long as you and your friends clean out the store."

The store was loaded from the floor to the ceiling with junk and rubbish, so my friends and me set to work to remove it all. After a thorough cleaning we painted the walls and the floor to give the place a new look. We washed the front windows and installed opaque tape on them.

After about two weeks when we finished all that work, me, Richie, and Johnny, were very happy and proud of our well-done job.

A week later, Patsy came across the street to look at our work.

"Well, fellas, you did a good job. The store looks brand new. I've changed my mind. I need the store for something more important than a clubhouse for kids."

I had to break this news to my friends. They went berserk on me. Richie yelled, "I hate your stupid father." The kicker was that they then accused me of being in on the scam.

"You really *are*," they shouted in unison, "a no good son-of-a-bitch!"

"This is my father's way," I told them. "He uses everyone he knows to get what he wants. He's the biggest con artist in the world!"

If they didn't believe me then, they did a couple of weeks later when he rented the store to a small-fry proprietor.

* * *

My friends' parents weren't as bad as Patsy. Richie and Johnny were richer in love and acceptance than I was; but in terms of actual money we were all equally broke. We never had any money to do things. This was long before the expensive sports clubs and supervised entertainment today's youth enjoy. We were self-entertained and under-funded.

One hot summer day we decided to go to the Aquacade which was a public pool near the World's Fair grounds in Flushing Meadows in Corona. A city bus ran up and down Corona Avenue to the park, but we never had money to take it.

On this particular day I said to Richie and Johnny, "Fellas, let's hitch a ride on the back of the bus." They agreed and we waited near the closest bus stop, trying not to look conspicuous. When the bus stopped, the three of us casually walked behind it and waited. As the bus left the stop, we jumped on and hung on by our fingernails to the hinge on the back of the bus with our feet turned out to the sides. We looked like ducks.

At successive stops we jumped off and on again.

Not only didn't we have money for the bus fare, we didn't have the quarter admittance fee to the Aquacade. But, as always, we found a way around this. We discovered that we could open up a side door to the pool and shimmy down a pipe which went to the locker room. There we changed into our bathing suits and spent the day swimming. We had the greatest time of our lives at the pool that summer.

I went off the ten-foot-high diving board, but Richie and Johnny were braver than I was. They dove off the forty-foot board. They climbed all the way up and did beautiful, perfect swan dives which were applauded by all the kids in the pool area.

***

When I was about thirteen years old, I got myself a job in an Italian bakery on 104th street. In Italian it was called *"Mangiare Pane,"* which in English means, "Eat bread"; but its English name was "Leonard's Bakery." I did the early morning bread deliveries with the bakery truck driver Pete and it was not easy work. I had to get up at 4:30 a.m. to deliver freshly baked warm bread. After working there for a while, I learned how to bake bread, rolling out the pre-cut dough and shaping it into balls to make loaves.

Margaret and Leonard owned the bakery. They had four children: Frankie; Lenny and Joey, who were twins; and their only daughter, Connie. The three sons were all boxers, and Lenny was even managed by the famous Rocky Graziano. The whole family was very kind to me. They fed me lunch every day I worked at the bakery, and I ate dinner with them sometimes on weekends. After we'd gotten to know each other well, they even brought me along on vacations with them to their big summer home in Connecticut. In the summer months we went there one weekend a month, and a full week in August. They were great people to work for, and I appreciated how they took me into their family.

After I got a minimum of experience, I was asked to work several hours at night to prepare the dough for the next day's baking. Margaret mustn't have known about this, for she wouldn't have approved. I did that for a while, but then I had to go home and get ready for school. I began to suffer from lack of sleep. It wasn't long before I had to call it quits, because I knew that if I wanted to be a baker, I'd have to work nights, and I just wasn't ready for that. To me days were for working and nights were for sleeping. To this day I have the deepest respect for all the people who work nights—firefighters, police, medical personnel, and transit workers.

CHAPTER 9

When I was thirteen my friends and me were hanging out at the candy store one day when a friendly young man casually walked over. He reached into his pocket as he greeted us and pulled out a yo-yo. He showed us the name on the yo-yo — "Duncan." He started doing some tricks with the yo-yo, and we were all impressed with how good he was. He told us that he worked for the Duncan Yo-Yo Company, and he wanted to know if we would be interested in learning some tricks on the yo-yo. The entire time he was talking the man never missed a beat doing yo-yo tricks. He took a break from his tricks and started handing out yo-yos to each of us. He showed us the simplest ones first: regular up-and-down; then, when we got the hang of that, he showed us how to make the yo-yo "sleep." All five of us guys stood there in front of the candy store trying to make our yo-yos sleep, and anyone passing by could tell that we were total amateurs.

The man said he'd be back the following week, and all week long instead of playing our regular street games we practiced with our yo-yos. Sure enough, he came back and again showed us a few more simple tricks, saying he'd be back again. We went home and practiced the tricks, and the following week the man showed us more difficult tricks. When he came back the fourth week, he announced that it was now time for a contest. When the neighborhood kids heard that, they all ran out and bought yo-yos and lined up to enter the contest. As the contest got in gear, one by one the kids in the neighborhood fell out.

That day I was the winner.

I was more surprised to have won than anyone else. I received a little patch for a jacket that said "Duncan Yo-Yo" on it.

As the weeks and months passed, the man came back every week, teaching us newer and harder tricks and sponsoring contests that became more and more competitive. I became very good with the yo-yo and won patch after patch, and then one day he came around with a bright yellow vest that had a big patch on the front that said, "Championship" on a big Duncan yo-yo emblem. I decided that day that I wanted to win that vest.

A short while later it became mine.

The tricks got MUCH harder. We mastered "The Cradle," in which you made the yo-yo go back and forth between your fingers like a swing. There was "The Dog Bite," where you'd throw the yo-yo between your legs and catch it in the crotch of your pants, and "The Pocket Trick," where you'd spread your legs apart for the yo-yo to go under your legs and then get it to go from behind into your pants' left pocket. Harder than that was "The Star," in which, throwing the yo-yo down, you formed a five-pointed star with it and then brought it back up.

One day the representative came around and said he was picking three kids from each borough for a contest in a big movie house in Jackson Heights the following Saturday morning. First prize would be a brand-new 1953 Chevy Bel Air. Two neighborhood boys and me were chosen from Queens.

We practiced all week long and the following Saturday morning me and my friends took the train to Jackson Heights. The contest began with fifteen kids on the stage. We started with tricks from the easiest to the most difficult one "The Star." The movie house was packed, and the whole first floor and the balcony were cheering sections for us. After the previous tricks were completed, the contest came down to three kids, two other boys and me.

In order to choose the winner, the judges assigned a "Loop-The-Loop" marathon, in which you threw the yo-yo out and when it came back, you looped it under your hand and threw it out again, repeatedly. The object was to do as many loops as you could. The one who did the most would be the winner.

The first boy completed about fifty loops before his yo-yo crashed. The next kid did ninety. I was last, so I knew I had to get more than that amount. I had confidence that I could do between a hundred and a hundred-fifty, so I concentrated on just beating ninety.

Right before I was about to start, one of my friends in the audience yelled up at me, "Bobby, change the string!" He knew that the yo-yo string had already been weakened. I was afraid, however, to change it because the string was all waxed up and the wax would stick to my fingers. I knew from experience that a new string would not cooperate the way I wanted it to.

Everyone in the audience was watching me. Kids and adults alike were screaming as I got ready to start my first loop. I threw my yo-yo out, getting ready to pull the string back, and at that moment of my very first try, the string broke sending my yo-yo flying out into the audience. I didn't even get a chance to complete one loop. The kid who did ninety loops won the car, the second-place winner got a trophy, and I wound up with a plaque.

* * *

Eighth grade was the final year at our elementary school. I was almost fifteen years old in eighth grade, two years older than most of the students in my class because of being left back twice. Everyone looked forward to graduation and especially the prom at the end of that year.

I approached Judy Nicolini, a pretty girl in my class. "Judy, will you go to the prom with me?"

"Yeah," she said, "I will."

Then something happened to kill my plans. One day near the end of eighth grade I was called to the principal's office. When I got there who did I see, but my friend Mikey Pennachio?

The principal looked very serious. "Bobby, you can't go to the prom."

My heart sank to the floor.

He said, "You're not going to graduate with the class of '55."

It turned out that Mikey and me hadn't been officially promoted in past years. For the nine years that we had been students our promotions to the next class had been conditional. Our promotions on report cards, in fact, were always recorded as "On condition." So, with no prom to go to,

Tommy Marino went with Barbara McQueire, and I took Judy Nicolini out to Patty's Restaurant in downtown Corona. I said, "Patty's is better than any old prom." Mikey hadn't asked a girl out, so he didn't come. There we were four young teenagers in a restaurant together without adults for the first time. We made our own prom that night, thumbing our noses at the school and it was a memorable night for all of us.

When I told Patsy that I wasn't going to graduate with the class, out came the strap and the beating began. I couldn't reach the bathroom that time to escape, so I had welts all over my legs and back. I think he was less angry that I wasn't graduating with the class than that he'd bought me a suit from Robert Hall's to wear for graduation. The store had altered it and he couldn't return it.

That same year Patsy decided to rebuild my grandfather's two-family house at 104-34 Corona Avenue. The construction under his supervision became a family affair. Engaged in the work were mainly Patsy, my brothers-in-law George and Mike, and me. We latter three had to listen to Patsy rant and rave about how we weren't doing what he wanted. All day long I had to listen to him say, "You stupid son-of-a-bitch, am I doing this for me? No, I'm doing it for you!"
This went on for weeks.

One day Tex , the youngest of the "four brothers," from the Four Brothers store came over to me and said, "Bobby, next time your father says that he's rebuilding this house for you tell him, 'Pop, you don't have to do this for me, I have a nice warm bed in my mother's house across the street where we live.'"

"That's all well and good," I answered. "But can't you see what will happen? My father will throw me out of my room."

Tex laughed.

You may wonder how an Italian boy got the nickname "Tex." The family name was Bianco. The oldest brother was Mike, then came Nick, then Joe, and the youngest was Anthony "Tex." When Tex had been a teenager, he took up the saxophone and played at block parties. At that time there was a well-known saxophone player named "Tex Beneke." Once a neighborhood guy called out to Anthony, "Hey, if it isn't Tex Beneke!" That was the moment my Italian friend from Corona got renamed "Tex." It didn't take long for us to forget that his real name was Anthony Bianco.

* * *

When I started public high school in 1955, I had to get medical clearance from a doctor who performed an examination on all incoming students. It was the most thorough examination I had ever had, and it revealed that I'd had an internal rupture at birth and that a part of my intestines was in my scrotum. At any point, I could have had an intestinal strangulation and died. When I heard that, I remember thinking that maybe that would have been better. The hernia operation was on the left side and I was glad to get it over with.

The following year I had a recurrence of the same hernia. This was getting tiresome. Again, I needed an operation. I was sixteen and had to go to the hospital for the repair. The surgeon, who was the best, operated.

Still and all I had a weak wall, and had to have the surgery again the next year on the right side. Patsy was fed up with me for the cost of hospitalization that his plan didn't cover. He made sure not to go with me so I went by myself.

The surgeon asked for the consent form to be signed by my parent since I was still a minor.

I heard the doctor say, "I won't perform this operation unless the form is signed."

A nurse told me, "You have to call your father to come immediately to the hospital to sign the consent form."

I called him. Patsy was enraged and came with great reluctance after my mother and sister begged him.

This was the straw that broke the camel's back. I was furious. From that time on we were bitter enemies.

In high school I formed a three-piece band and we had a gig one Friday night a month at the V.F.W. Post hall. Each of us got $5 for the night.

I felt very rich and started to buy some nice clothes for high school at Clapper's, a clothing store in our neighborhood. I was the best-dressed guy at school with a new outfit every day. Most of my fellow students didn't dress very good and I was the talk of my high school.

But I had not yet learned that clothes do not always make the man. One day in school I was acting up, totally out of control, and the teacher sent me to the principal's office. Mr. Bundle, the principal, said, "Mr. Lauri your disruptive behavior in school requires that I bring your father in to put a stop to it."

"My father is working in the plumbing trade," I told Mr. Bundle, "and if he has to leave work for half a day, he won't get paid."

But that wasn't Mr. Bundle's concern; the call was made and Patsy arrived at the school that same afternoon. As soon as Mr. Bundle and Mr. Weinberger, the assistant principal, began telling him how bad my behavior in school was, Patsy immediately began beating me right in front of them, chasing me all around the principal's office. Mr. Bundle and Mr. Weinberger were so upset that they stood against the wall in shock and amazement with their eyes bulging out of their heads. After my father had gone, the two administrators promised me that they would never call my father up to school again. I continued getting into trouble at school but at least, after that, the trouble didn't follow me home.

I had thought that in high school I might turn over a new leaf and have a fresh start, but what I didn't know yet was the old expression, "No matter where you go, your problems go with you."

My self-esteem had long since been beaten out of me. I had no confidence in myself. I felt like a dummy, coming out of primary school barely able to read or write. In high school there were fights every day at the school or around the school area. Kids tried to extort money out of younger, weaker kids, and if you weren't strong enough to stand up to them they stole your lunch money. I had to defend myself in some way every day, but at least dealing with my father had prepared me to constantly be alert to threats.

Students were given authority over one another, such as in monitoring the gym doors. The monitor was not allowed to let anyone through the gym once class started, but students tried to cut through to make it to their next class on time. When I was a monitor, I let kids go through the door when they were late and Dr. Hartley, the gym teacher, yelled at me from the gym floor, "Lauri, keep that door closed!"

One day a six-foot tall, lanky guy, who I nicknamed "Lanky", was monitoring the doors and me and a few classmates wanted to go through the gym to the next class. With that, "Lanky" demanded money. My fellow classmates decided that it was not worth making a scene, and they left. I didn't. I asked "Lanky" if I could go through without being shaken down and giving him my lunch money. *I mean, how was I supposed to get that tuna fish sandwich from Mom's Luncheonette across the street from the school if I gave this guy my money?* I saw, since he wasn't backing down, only one way to solve the problem. So at five-foot-eight, I decked 'Mr. Six-Foot-Two' with all my might. One punch from my right hand and I saw the blood from his face all over the gym floor. Dr. Hartley came over and grabbed me, and said, "What did you do to this kid?"

The tall guy kept bleeding. I said, "Dr. Hartley, he was shaking down all the kids for money to go through the gym to the next class and this has been going on for a long time. He stopped the wrong guy this morning."

Needless to say, "Lanky" was removed from monitoring the door and suspended from school for a while. I never had trouble with him again

I was definitely not one of the studious kids in school and just as it had been in elementary school, if there was a prank or a disruption, I was likely involved. One day our English teacher, Mrs. Shackleton, asked if anyone would like to move some books from the school library to the book depository on the fourth floor. A few of my classmates and me volunteered. Mrs. Shackleton also mentioned that we were going to get a commendation for volunteering. I asked her what we were going to use to move the books; we had no dollies or a wagon to put the books in. I came up with the idea of using a dumpster from the lunch room. I went to the lunch room to get the dumpster and went back to the library and started to fill the dumpster up with books. About seven or eight of us made a few trips back and forth moving books until it got really boring.

So, I came up with a way to have some fun. On the way to the book room we were wheeling the dumpster loaded with books to the freight elevator and I decided to take the stairs. My classmates thought I was crazy. Why would we push a full dumpster up four flights of stairs? But down was what I had in mind. Halfway up the first level I pushed the loaded dumpster down the stairs. Even a whisper echoed in those stairwells, so you can just imagine the racket those books in the dumpster made flying down the stairs. You would have thought we'd detonated a bomb. My classmates and me laughed so hard we got stomach pains. That was the end of my volunteering career.

That same year I had a teacher named Miss Connelly. I drove that teacher so nuts that she almost had a nervous breakdown. I behaved so badly that I even made her cry. She sent me to the principal's office and they gave me detention, but the next day in Miss Connelly's class I went right back to harassing her.

That semester Miss Connelly was accepted to be on a popular television game show. All the contestants were put in a soundproof bubble, and when Miss Connelly was in the bubble she had to answer questions. I don't remember what categories she chose, but she answered her questions correctly and wound up winning $8,000. She also won a date with Richard Egan, a very handsome actor at the time.

Miss Connelly was back in class on Monday and everyone in the class wanted to hear about the date, but she wouldn't talk about it. Class went on as usual. I knew I could make her angry with me, so I kept cutting up in class, being as bad as ever. But for once, it had no effect on her. That was her last day teaching our class; we heard she gave notice and quit her teaching job because she was able to live off the prize money she'd won. I don't remember how long after the program had been on television it was discovered to have been fraudulent. According to the media and newspaper stories about it, the contestants were given hints about the correct answers. Who knows if that's how Miss Connelly won, but by then it didn't really matter.

Miss Connelly's class was English 4. High school English classes were numbered from one through eight; we had two classes per year. At the beginning of my final term in my senior year, I thought I'd finished English 7, but I was in for a surprise. I looked at my new program card for the eighth term and saw that every subject had an eighth term class assigned, but as I glanced down to the bottom, it said "English 1" with a freshman room number. I had somehow missed that class, or had failed it and didn't even remember, and all I could think about was how embarrassing it would be to be in a class with all freshmen. But it was what it was. I still needed the class to graduate.

I decided to make peace with myself and make the best of it. I went to all my classes the first day, and eighth period, the last class of the day, was Freshman English 1. The bell rang, and I was a little late getting to the classroom. When I walked in, almost all the seats were full and before I could even find a seat, the teacher showed me right back to the door. Why? Because that English 1 teacher was Miss Connelly. I hadn't known she was back, but she remembered me and wasn't going to allow me to take that class. She told me to go to my school advisor and ask to be put in another English class.

I went to the advisor, Miss Clair, who told me that Miss Connelly's was the only English 1 class that semester and that without that class I couldn't graduate. What was I to do? My class-clown ways had caught up with me. I went back to Miss Connelly's class and begged her to let me stay, explaining that Miss Clair had said that taking it was my only way to graduate. I was completely at her mercy.

Miss Connelly gazed at me, her face stern, and said, "Look into my eyes, and do not take your eyes off of them until I am done speaking to you. I'll let you stay in my class with three conditions. One: You must take the last row and last seat in the last row and you must be quiet. Two: I don't want you to engage in any class activity. No schoolwork, no homework, nothing.

Three: You keep your mouth shut for the next six months, and I will give you a grade of sixty-five just to let you pass so you'll be able to graduate. Do you understand what I am saying to you?"

I smiled and said, "I do," and that was exactly what I did for the next six months. No speaking in class, no interacting with other students. She had remembered everything I did in her other class, and this was my penalty. At the end of the class year, I remember she gave me a hug and said, "I hope you find in life what you are looking for."

After having done little more in school since the first grade than act as class clown, I never developed an interest in reading and I read very little. Throughout high school I never even carried books. Those four years consisted of my going from one class to another with a pencil. But I graduated high school with almost an 80 average, more by means of strength and cunning than through hard work and academic skill.

CHAPTER 10

Harman's ice cream parlor near the high school was the hangout after school for students to have soda and French fries. My neighborhood was mostly Italian, but my high school had many Jewish students, and I had a lot of Jewish friends who hung out at Harman's. That's where I learned that Jewish people and Italians have a lot in common.

One day Linda Goldberg, Ruth Helm, and Louie Segal, all really good students, asked me to help them with a bunch of young punks who used to rip up their homework. I arranged with them that if they would help me with my schoolwork and write book reports for me from time to time, I would deal with those punks. I was a good fighter and thus for the rest of my high school career I got into many fights to keep the peace for my friends. These friends of mine were very smart, with 85 to 90 averages, and they didn't just do my work for me. They helped me study and they were excellent tutors. They helped me understand the work better than I had before. By the end of high school, I graduated with a 79.9 average.

* * *

Back in the 1940's when I was growing up most weddings were called "football weddings." All of the tables had different kinds of sandwiches on them and if you didn't see one you liked on your table, you'd yell across the wedding hall to see if the other tables had different ones, "You got ham over there?"

Someone would throw it over to you like a football. They were heavy sandwiches, too. When it was time for dessert, men would volunteer to walk around the hall to each table with a big tray of cream puffs and cookies. At the bottom of the pile of desserts on the tray were "confetti," candied almonds of every color. My teeth hurt and I couldn't eat them.

I rarely went to the dentist when I was growing up. One of the few times I did go, in fact, was when an abscess developed under a tooth and the tooth had to be extracted. My sister Nancy brought me to Dr. Cromer, an excellent dentist, and when I walked into his office screaming with pain, he took one look in my mouth and, with an angry look on his face, said to my sister, "How could a family let a child go this long without an exam? You people should be ashamed of yourselves!"

Dr. Cromer pulled the tooth. The procedure hurt like hell.

* * *

From the time I was little you'd find me sitting by the band watching the drummer at every family wedding. I loved music and I loved the drums. I wanted to play the drums more than anything, even more than I wanted a bike. When I was about ten years old, I finally told my father that I wanted to play the drums. He immediately started yelling at me, "Ya outta your mind? Ya want the tenants to move out? What'll we do then with no rent comin' in?"

But when he found out that my cousin Ronnie was learning the accordion, he made a deal with the teacher and that's how I started taking accordion lessons, which was better than nothing. My grandfather agreed to pay for my lessons–$2.50 an hour. I had lessons once a week, and every day when I wasn't practicing, I listened to the popular songs of the day on the radio. The songs now thought of as 40's and 50's classics—by Frank Sinatra, Nat King Cole, Tony Bennett, Patty Page—were the top pop hits at that time.

Once a week, Mr. Stebner, my music teacher, brought me the sheet music for whatever song was number one on that week's top ten list. When I started playing the song, Mr. Stebner noticed that I wasn't looking at the sheet music, yet I was playing that song perfectly note for note by ear. Every week it was the same thing. One week the song was "Because of You" by Tony Bennett. Another week it was "Goodnight, Irene." Mr. Stebner was amazed; he couldn't understand how I played the songs without reading the notes. He finally asked me how I managed to do it.

"I listen to the radio every day. They play the same songs over and over, so every time I hear them I sing along to the melody and then I accompany the song on the accordion instead of singing it."

It was at that moment that Mr. Stebner realized I had "echoic memory," or the equivalent of photographic memory for sound. I could play just about anything by ear. If you asked me to play a C-scale, I knew right where to start. I was able to play every song I'd heard on the radio or on a phonograph record after hearing it a couple of times.

My musical ear could find pitch and key as well. There was a piano in my elementary school auditorium. One day a man came into the auditorium with a little case in his hand and he went over to the piano. As I watched, he took some sort of a wrench and a piece of equipment that looked like a two-pronged fork out of his little case. Later I learned it was called a "tuning fork." He started to play the piano keys one at a time and then he hit his tuning fork with a metal rod. As he tuned that piano in the auditorium, I listened carefully. I could feel in my ear just about when he was reaching the right pitch on the key.

I walked over and asked the man if I could tune the piano with him. He smiled at me and I said to him, "I play the accordion, why don't you hit <A> on the piano and let me see if I can tune the <A> key without the tuning fork."

His smile got even bigger and as he put the tuning wrench on the <A> string in the piano and started hitting the <A> key, he said, "Go ahead, kid."

I could tell by my ear that the <A> key was very much off. The man kept looking at me and I told him to turn the wrench a little more, a little more, and then some. I listened ever more intently until I said, "Stop!"

He looked at me with that smile again as he picked up the tuning fork and hit the   <A> key. It was in perfect pitch. His smile turned to amazement, and he said, "Let's try another key." Again, without the tuning fork he with his wrench and me with my ear tuned that key to perfect pitch.

"Kid," he said, "you have something that not too many people have."

"What's that?" I asked him.

"You've got a perfect 4-40 pitch," he said. "If I didn't see you do this with my own eyes, and hear you do this with my own ears, I wouldn't have believed it."

This must be why I can to this day play on both the accordion and the piano almost any song I've heard. I also can pick out a wrong chord in a song I hear on the radio. That doesn't happen often, but it does with one particular Christmas song. Some orchestrations get it right and some get it wrong. Most people don't detect the difference, but I can always tell.

One day during my accordion lesson, Patsy asked Mr. Stebner, my music teacher, what the best European-made accordion was. "The Dallapé," he replied. "In the United States that accordion is worth $1500, but you can get one in Europe for about $500."

"Are you thinking of buying that accordion for Bobby?" asked Mr. Stebner.

"Yes," answered my father, "my neighbor is leaving for a vacation in Europe."

"Well, it will cost you about five hundred, but remember, you have to get a black one for it to be worth more here."

I had been playing on a small 48-bass accordion. The Dallapé was a 120-bass. Patsy went and spoke with our neighbor Tex. He asked him to bring back the accordion, and Tex agreed after Patsy gave him the money.

I was in shock. Patsy never did nice things like that for me. Tex went to Europe and found the Dallapé accordion factory in Stradella, Italy, and bought an accordion for $500.

The story wasn't that simple. At that time the factory had only a white accordion for sale. Tex didn't know what to do; he had to make a quick decision whether or not to purchase the white accordion. He remembered, of course, that Patsy had specified that he wanted a black one. Patsy hadn't mentioned to Tex that there would be a problem if he brought back one of a different color, so Tex thought that he had some discretion in the matter. Being that he had gone all the way to Italy, he figured that getting such a great deal for an accordion worth $1500 in the United States was better than getting no accordion at all. So, he bought the white accordion.

Tex returned from Europe a few weeks later and gave Patsy the accordion. When Patsy opened the case and saw that the accordion was white, his face turned red and he started screaming at poor Tex, "I told you I wanted a black accordion!"

Tex told him about the on-the-spot decision he'd had to make. "The sales rep there told me that they'd have a black accordion in a couple of weeks, but I wasn't going to be there then so I figured a white accordion was better than no accordion at all!"

As I grew older, I figured out what may have been behind Patsy's decision to spend all that money on the Dallapé. Giving him the benefit of the doubt, perhaps he was thinking of me as a kind of musician "cash cow." I think, more probably, he may have had in mind that if I stopped playing the accordion at some point, he'd be able to sell the accordion at a profit. Even the white accordion he may have figured he'd eventually be able to sell at about $1,000, perhaps to Mr. Stebner, my accordion teacher. But when Mr. Stebner opened the case and saw a white accordion, he wanted no part of it.

After that, Patsy saw Tex on the street corner one day and argued with him again about it. Poor Tex told Patsy, "I carried that accordion with me on my whole vacation! I was afraid to leave it anywhere, even at the hotel where I was staying. I feared it would get stolen. This is the thanks I get?"

CHAPTER 11

I did soften up a bit when it came to my father. I don't know how I came to have so many operations but once again I needed surgery. When I had a pyonital cyst on my tailbone or in medical terms, my coccyx. I was really surprised when Patsy came without backtalk and signed the consent form willingly.

I was hospitalized for ten days and five days later I was shocked to see Patsy come in with a big smile. I knew he was up to something. He wanted to borrow money. He was a con man if I ever saw one.

After a cold "Hello" he said, "I need a loan of $500 to buy a new Chrysler Windsor."

"Yeah. Okay. When I get out of the hospital I'll go to the bank and get you the money."

I remembered the $500 he'd paid for the Dallapé accordion. I figured out that he had had an ulterior motive for requesting the $500 loan; he wanted to be reimbursed for the accordion. He had had the money to pay cash for the car. Since I figured I would never see that $500 again, I thought I would be able to at least use the car during the day while Patsy was at work.

One day while me and my friends were cruising around the neighborhood, one of my friends came up with the idea of taking a ride to Rockaway Beach. So off we went and had a grand time. When I returned home and gave Patsy the keys to the car, he went right down to where I'd parked it, and checked the mileage on the odometer.

He came back up to the house, shouting, "You son-of-a-bitch, you put a hundred miles on it in one day!"

He pissed me off, and that was the end of my driving Patsy's car.

Paying all that money for the Dallapé must have made Patsy feel that he was entitled to be entertained by it at his whim. Every time we had company he had me play the accordion for them. When I didn't, he took it away from me for months at a time.

There came a time when the family was invited to my cousin's wedding.

Patsy whispered, "I expect you to play at the wedding."

"This time I won't."

Patsy bit down hard on his lips. He grabbed the accordion and took it away.

At that moment I decided I'd had enough. I stormed out of our apartment, and the next thing I saw was all my clothing being thrown out of our second-floor window.

"Don't come back!" he shouted down to me.

I was eighteen years old and homeless. I went to stay with my friend Tony Mangano, and I wound up living with Tony for a few months until I could afford to rent a furnished room in Flushing.

At the end of the fifties rock-and-roll was starting to edge out the classic crooners like Frank Sinatra, Tony Bennett, Vic Damone, and Peggy Lee, who sang from the *American Song Book* songs written by Cole Porter, Irving Berlin, and George and Ira Gershwin. While in high school, I wrote a rock-and-roll song called "Blind Date" with two of my friends Ronnie Tamborri and Peter Balducci.

One of the biggest record producers of that time was Bernie Lowe. In 1955 this man produced more rock-and-roll records than anybody featuring different artists. As the producer he invested his money in the projects and paid for all the music arrangements and recording studio time. He could make a profit if one or two of fifteen songs became a hit. It was a risky business, but Bernie did well.

He had been recruiting in high schools all over New York City and when he heard about our band, he came to our rehearsal, which was at a makeshift studio that doubled as a TV repair shop. At that time rock-and-roll singles featured three or four guys singing doo-wop harmony, just like the classic doo-wop guys who hung out on the street corners harmonizing.

For our record, four young aspiring singers sang the song we'd written so Bernie could hear it. He liked it and agreed to produce it.

Before long, it was all over school that we were going to cut a record for the CBS record company.

We recorded our single at Bell Sound Studios in Manhattan with members of the Musicians Union Local 802. Bernie had gotten some of the best musicians in the industry to the recording session: King Curtis, one of the top sax players in rock-and-roll history, and Freddy Cole on piano, who was the brother of Nat King Cole and uncle to Natalie Cole, both famous, smooth-voiced singers.

Before we started to do the first take, King Curtis asked Bernie Lowe if there were any guys playing in this session who did not belong to Local 802. Bernie didn't know what to say. He asked me if I was in the union. I lied that I was only fifteen years old and added that I didn't know anything about unions. The band wouldn't start the session. So, King Curtis and Freddy Cole told Bernie, "Take these guys to 802, sign 'em up, and come back. Then we'll start the session."

Bernie was paying for the studio time so he hurried me, my guitar player, and my bass player over to Local 802 headquarters. I paid $55, which Bernie gave me, to join the musician's union. I still remember my card number – L3595. My card read, "Robert Lauri, member of Local 802," with the card number next to my name. I felt proud to be a member.

We went back to the studio, and what a session we had playing with those top musicians. King Curtis was one of the best honky-tonk players in the business, with that deep sound coming out of the bell of his saxophone. But even though me and my friends were now union members, we didn't get paid for the recording session and we never heard from Bernie Lowe again. I guess our record didn't make the grade. Our recording days were over before they'd barely begun.

When I was eighteen, I got a call from my old band mate Ronnie Tamborri. Gil Galante needed an accordion player to work a nightclub in Astoria, The Old Homestead. Gil was a great guitar player and he used to give lessons to Ronnie. I told Ronnie I would do the gig, which was from 9 p.m. until 3 a.m. I was so tired that I barely made it through the night. What a star I was! I was paid $12.50 a night and given a free salami sandwich. Such was my gig!

Eventually, we got hired to play a gig at the Holiday Inn in Flushing. My trio consisted of me on accordion, Gil Galante on the guitar, and Frankie Valente on bass. Working opposite us was a big band led by Bobby Madera. That gig got us in the door, and we were called back to play there again. By 1960 we played there regularly. We played unusually short sets, twenty minutes on and forty off, because we were just filling in for the dance band.

We sometimes worked with a dance band led by a man named Tito Puente. I worked with Tito Puente for a long time, and as he was the leader of his band and I was the leader of mine, we met before shows to go over schedules. We worked around two dancers, the local area stars Mike and Joan Parker. Nobody could do the Latin dances like those two.

Frequently I went into the city in the morning to take care of union business, and I used to go to a coffee shop on Seventh Avenue where all the local musicians met to shoot the breeze. In today's world people would call this "networking." I had my breakfast at the counter where there were seven seats, usually all full.

One morning after finishing my breakfast, I asked the waitress for my check and she told me that the check had already been taken care of. I looked down the counter to see who had picked up my check and saw "the one and only" Tito Puente leaning his head over and giving me a big smile.

My trio, as I said, often played our steady weekends at the Holiday Inn with Tito Puente's band. I went over to greet Tito with a big "Hello" and "Thank you!" We chatted for a few minutes and before I left, Tito told me, "I'll see you Friday night."

"God willing!"

One weekend in the 1960's the owner of the Holiday Inn, Mrs. Abbott, wanted to try something new and add a star to the show, so she hired Frank Sinatra, Jr., to sing. As the show was getting under way, Frank Sinatra, Jr., came out to perform and as soon as he started to sing, the crowd went berserk, but not in a good way. They didn't care who his father was; they booed this poor guy who was just trying to entertain them. I'd been booed off a stage before, so I knew how he must have felt, and I felt bad for him. Some guys who'd had too many drinks started to throw bottles on the dance floor and when he left the stage to go to his dressing room, I went down to see him.

I said, "I'm real sorry that you were treated lousy. I don't think you should go on anymore because the angry crowd is getting drunker by the minute."

I guess the crowd must have felt he was trying to milk the "Sinatra" name. He took my advice. After Frank Sinatra, Jr., left the Holiday Inn that night, I didn't see him again for a long while.

* * *

After I had graduated from high school in 1958, I had gone to work for an insurance company in Manhattan for $35 a week. It wasn't very long before I realized that I hated the job. I'd thought that by having a high school diploma, I'd be working in a nice office behind a desk learning the insurance business, but that wasn't the case at all. Instead, the manager put me in the basement with another guy and all day long the only thing we did was prepare different types of insurance forms.

I didn't see any sort of future there for myself, but I remembered that I'd known the plumbing trade from working with Patsy, so I left the insurance job and joined the Plumbers' Union. The union treasurer was Michael Sazarulla, and I asked Michael what the initiation fee was to join the union and he told me, "$125."

I paid him the fee, and he handed me a temporary union card and said, "Tomorrow morning you're going to a job in the city."

That first week on the job I made $65, almost doubling the salary that I'd made at the insurance company in the basement. I was supposed to go through a five-year plumbers' apprentice program, and after I'd been in three years, the construction industry got very busy, with many out-of-town plumbers coming in to work on jobs around the city. I went on to mechanics' work.

One of the bosses, Bernie Wachtel, approached me on the job and said, "Mr. Lauri, if you go down to the union and get a letter of approval to make mechanics' wages, I'll increase your salary to what a journeyman plumber makes."

I went down to union headquarters and got the approval letter, and the following week my salary jumped up to $175 a week. I had started out in 1959 as an apprentice plumber and then worked my way up to journeyman working on various building projects throughout the city.

One particular place where I worked was the Women's Detention Center on Riker's Island. My partner at that time was Leroy Diamond, who I knew as "Lee." I worked with him for about three and a half years.

One day Lee asked me if I would drive him to Fort Schuyler in the Bronx that evening and I said, "Sure, I'd love to."

Lee met me at my house in Queens and we left from there. As we drove to the nineteenth-century fort near the Throgs Neck Bridge, he told me that we were going to have dinner there.

When we arrived at Ft. Schuyler, a U.S. Marine Corps soldier escorted us to our table. At that moment I noticed that the banquet hall was filled with Marine Corps officers in their dress uniforms, with gold braid on their hats and sleeves. They all approached Lee and saluted him, one big brass after another. I knew that the gold leaf on the arm of their uniforms meant that these were admirals and other high ranking Marine officers. I was startled, and after they all filed away, I asked Lee, "What have I just seen? Why are all these officers saluting you?"

Lee just shrugged it off and wouldn't tell me. I let it go, and even as we drove home that night, I decided I didn't want to question him about it.

The next day I was relocated to a different job on the East Side. I didn't see Lee again for a few years until we met again at a job site. We were teamed up as partners. I reminded him about the dinner at Fort Schuyler, and I asked him again, "Why did all those high-ranking officers salute you that night?" But Lee still held back.

Around that time some workers came around to different job sites agitating in the hope of creating job openings. We got word that protesters were coming to disrupt our work. We were told by our foreman to drop our tools and just stand in place. As we stood there, Lee came over to me holding a paper bag in his hand. He handed it to me. I opened it and saw that it was full of medals. I began pulling the medals out one by one, not knowing what any of them meant. I asked Lee, and he told me: one was a Purple Heart, one was a Navy Cross. He also had numerous ribbons. One had little colored bars above a medal. Lee said it was for action in the war.

As we workers stood there waiting for the protesters to leave, Lee told me about a movie called *The Pride of the Marines*. I said that I knew that movie because, in addition to my having seen it, my brother-in-law Sal was a movie buff and had talked about it many times. Lee then explained that that movie showed some of *his* war experiences. He told me that Dane Clark played *him* and John Garfield played Al Schmitt. I couldn't believe that in all the years I was teamed up with Lee on the job, he'd never said a word about what took place overseas and in the Pacific. In the critical scene of *The Pride of the Marines*," Leroy is feeding Schmitt the ammunition for the machine gun. At that moment Schmitt gets hit with shrapnel in his eye and goes momentarily blind. Leroy then takes the machine gun and starts to fire at all the Japanese coming at him. He kills many of the enemy.

To this day I am amazed and filled with pride to have spent as much time as I did in the company of such a humble and heroic man. No wonder the top brass saluted him at that dinner at Fort Schuyler. All Lee said about it at the construction site was, "Bobby, I was in the right place at the right time."

After working in the plumbing field for eight years I decided to change my career, and in 1967 I became a thermostat man working for Metro Control. My first job was at the Louis Rudin Building in midtown Manhattan, a huge fifty-story building.

The first morning on the job I met my foreman Freddy Reef, a real gentleman. Since I was the first man on the job, the union delegate appointed me shop steward. My union business agent was Henry Murray. He was the brother of John Murray, who at that time was the President of Local #2 of the Plumbers Union. Freddie Reef was the one who really taught me the temperature-control business.

Another employee I worked with was Bobby Farina. He ran the service department.

A few years later Bobby asked me to come and work for him. He was one of the nicest guys you ever wanted to meet. He taught me how to set up the controls, but there were just certain things I couldn't seem to remember in setting up a control system and he told me over and over again, "Bobby, if you can play the accordion the way you do, then this thing should be a piece of cake."

The head of Metro Control, Mr. Conway, threw a big company Christmas party every year and he always asked me to entertain with my accordion. Bobby Farina had always wanted to be a singer. He had a beautiful voice and he sang at these Christmas parties to my accordion accompaniment. I truly loved this guy and I always respected him, particularly for one thing: he handled subordinates with style. He was the only supervisor who never listened to any of the gossip or stories that the other employees brought to him about me. If he heard a rumor that I might have said something wrong to an account representative in the course of the day, he always brought it to me first. He'd say to me, "Bobby, so-and-so said that you were out of order with such-and-such a person," and he would tell me what he'd heard.

I appreciated that so much that I would tell him the honest truth if I had done or said anything questionable. But most of the time it was false accusations and office politics, which, unfortunately, goes on in organizations. He dropped the matter right then and there and never brought it up to me again. That's the kind of man Bobby Farina was.

CHAPTER 12

One Friday it was "Latin Night" at the Holiday Inn night club. I was working with my trio and admiring Tito's band. I had been playing weekends there for a while by then, but that night three new girls came into the club. I later learned their names, Anne, Jacqueline, and Mary.

As I was getting off the stage, Ann walked over to me. "Do you know if "Bow-legged Joe" has been here? He's supposed to meet me and repay the $200 I gave him."

"I never heard of that guy."

I noticed one of the other girls who was with her, the one named Jacqueline. She had large beautiful hazel eyes, and she looked like a movie star.

I joined the girls in a booth near the bar, Anne and Mary sat on one side of the table and Jacqueline and me on the other. As I was talking to Jacqueline, I noticed that she was clinging to my arm and stealing long glances at me when she thought I wasn't noticing. Then she said something kind, "Try and save your money because it looks like you're working real hard standing up on stage and playing."

After some more small talk the three girls left, and I went over to the bar to hang out with a couple of friends of mine and some girls who were with them. I thought one of the girls was giving me dirty looks and, for the life of me, I couldn't imagine why.

The following weekend this girl was back at the bar and giving me the stink-eye again. But this time I found out why. "Why are you annoyed with me?"

"I seen you sitting in the booth, flirting with Jacqueline last week. I'm Lana and Jacqueline is my cousin and she's only sixteen." That was interesting.

"Jacqueline told me she was eighteen."

Lana was wearing a beautiful black dress that went well with her black hair. I thought she looked fantastic. I had to go up and play a set, but I decided I was going to ask her out.

The next night, while Tito Puente was playing, I noticed that Jacqueline and her friend Anne were back. I went over to say hello, took one look at Jacqueline, and completely forgot about her cousin. I fell for her at that moment. When I got onstage and started to play my set, I noticed that Jacqueline was dancing the "Paso Doble" with Barney, an older man.

So as I watched the two of them dance, I realized that I was burning with jealousy.

When I came off the stage, I walked over to Jacqueline. After everything I'd been through in my life, I wasn't the type to let my guard down. I knew that Jacqueline was different than anyone I'd ever met. I had to speak up. "Jacqueline I'm jealous about your dancing with Barney."

"You don't have to be jealous. Barney works for my father in his plant that distributes sawdust. He's like a second father to me."

"That's different," I said. "I'd like your phone number."

"It's a long story but I just can't give it to you."

"Okay, I'll give you my number. Call me tomorrow."

The next day I didn't think she would call but when she did I said, "I'd like to take you to a little Chinese restaurant across the street from the club. We can go during my break."

She agreed and when we went there we found that the restaurant had space for only ten people. That was all right with the both of us. We got to talk a lot. This was in February of 1960. By the end of March we were going steady.

After two years we got engaged. I was twenty-two years old and Jacqueline was eighteen.

One week I worked the Copacabana Lounge with a drummer named Philly Yorker. It was only for a week, but in that short time I explored the whole place, from the showroom to the kitchen. The owner of the Copa was Jules Pardel and he always sat at a table on the left side of the club. When we finished our show in the lounge, Philly Yorker, who was also the bandleader, told me, "Bobby, you need to exit the stage from the right side, not the left side."

I never questioned it. I just followed directions.

ME AND JACQUELINE AT THE COPA

That week the famous Tom Jones was appearing in the showroom downstairs. The line for his show went down the street and around the corner. I called Jacqueline from work and asked her if she wanted to see Tom Jones.

"Are you crazy? I saw on TV that there are lines around the block to get into that show!"

"Don't worry. Just come down tomorrow and I'll get you in."

The following night she came to the Copa and waited in line outside the club. I knew how to get her into the showroom through the kitchen. I was waiting for her at the front of the Knobby Walters' Club next door to the Copa. Lou Walters was the owner who had once owned the Latin Quarter, another famous night club.

I spotted Jacqueline waiting in line. I waved to her but she was so nervous she wasn't even looking around for me. The woman standing next to her nudged her and said, "That fellow is trying to get your attention."

Jacqueline reluctantly left her place in line and walked toward me. I took her by the hand and we went downstairs to the kitchen in the basement. We snuck through the hectic commotion of the kitchen, where we passed all the chefs and wait staff on our way into the showroom. The *maitre'd* motioned to us to follow the captain who showed us to our table in front of stage. The regular guests were coming down the stairs from the main entrance into the showroom at the same time, and a man shouted, "How does that guy get a table up front?"

Many years later there was a famous scene in a movie that reenacted the same situation. Every time Jacqueline and me watched that movie we got a kick out of the scene where the characters Henry and his date Karen walk through the kitchen of the Copa, just as we had done years earlier. That is a very special memory for us because it was the beginning of our romance.

After we got engaged we had to have an engagement party. Jacqueline and me had both saved a little money, and we wanted to have it at Tofaro's Restaurant in Corona. But when we put our funds together, we found that we didn't have enough. I knew Rudy Tofaro, the owner of the restaurant, very well from the neighborhood and he told us that if we could come up with a little more money, he'd give us a good deal for the party. A light bulb went off in my head and I remembered the $500 I'd "loaned" Patsy for his car, so I decided it was time to ask him to pay me back.

That did not go well. Patsy got very angry at me for asking, and the conversation ended abruptly. That was the end of that. I felt like nailing his ass.

A few weeks later Jacqueline and me stopped in to have a cup of coffee with my sister Nancy in Corona. As we walked into Nancy's apartment, I noticed a fruit bowl on the kitchen table that had a piece of paper in it. It was a check for $500 made out to me and signed by Patsy.

He'd had second thoughts about repaying me, but I knew he hated doing it and couldn't bring himself to hand me the check and thank me in person for the loan. The outside world, neighbors and acquaintances, rarely saw that miserly side of him. He was a great guy to those who didn't know him well, inviting neighbors over to eat his cheese and the *prosciutto* that he cured in the basement and to drink his homemade wine. They thought he was a generous *"compadre,"* a *"goombah."* But his family knew that on the inside he was unbelievably stingy and cruel.

At 3 a.m. I left work and walked from the subway station on my way home. In the pitch dark I saw cops all over Corona Avenue and yellow crime scene tape stretching from Quacky's candy store and the barbershop next to it, all around the light poles in front.

I went over to one of the plainclothes police officers at the scene. "What's going on?"

"Yesterday there was a shooting."

"Is that so? I work in the candy store once in a while and help Quacky out with cleaning up the place. Can you tell me who was involved?"

"The owner of the candy store shot two people."

"It can't be. I've known that man my whole life. When I was a kid, I used to help him clean the store, wipe the counters, and put the cigarettes on the shelves."

"Well, Frank DeVito, the owner of the candy store has been arrested and he's in the precinct lockup."

That was the first time I'd ever heard Quacky's real name. I started to walk away and crossed the street to go home to my apartment but I changed my mind. I turned around and went back to speak to the detective again.

"How do you know it was Quacky who shot those two fellows?"

"Because after the shooting, Quacky called the police and told them he shot two people who were robbing him for the second time. When the officers came he gave them the gun he used to shoot them."

Later I learned the whole story. Frank DeVito owned his candy store for years. Everyone in the neighborhood knew him as "Quacky" and his store didn't really sell much candy, mostly cigars, cigarettes, and newspapers. When the shooting happened, Quacky was eighty years old and the whole neighborhood knew and loved him. For years Quacky's steady customers came in on Sunday mornings. He sold them wine in back of the store for a quarter a glass. His regulars were very content to sit at a table in the back, drinking and making small talk about what went on in the neighborhood that week.

One Sunday a couple of weeks before the shooting a few of the guys got rowdy and picked a fight with Quacky. Anthony was one of these guys and he and another guy went to the front of the store and started stealing Quacky's cigars and cigarettes from behind the counter. When Quacky yelled at them to stop, they started beating the hell out of him.

The next day I stopped into the candy store to buy my newspaper, as I always did. But when I saw Quacky's bruised and beaten face, all black and blue, I felt like a mad dog. I asked him, "Who the hell in the world did this to you?"

Quacky was originally from Italy, and when he came over he didn't learn English very good. He answered me in his broken English, "Bobby, some men beata me up anna stole all my cigarette and cigar from behin' the counter."

"Did you call the police?"

"Naw, don-na worry about it, Bobby. I take-a care of everythin'."

The following Sunday the same two guys came into the candy store for their usual twenty-five cent glasses of wine. That's the kind of guy Quacky was, forgiving, loving everyone, and even willing to give the guys another chance who had stolen from him and hurt him.

After a few hours of drinking the same things started to happen all over again: the men got rowdy and yelled at Quacky, probably with the same thing on their mind as the last time—stealing from his store.

Quacky shouted at them in his broken English, "Whatta you doing? Again-ya steal from me?" From behind the counter he started throwing cigar boxes at them. Cigars were all over the floor. He grabbed the cigars from six boxes at them and hurled them. When he got to the last box, he opened it up and pulled out a gun that was hidden in it.

The two guys, drunk and intent on robbery, didn't notice the gun until Quacky came behind the counter and chased them out of his store, taking a shot at one guy as he ran up Corona Avenue. He shot the other guy as he ran around the corner and the guy fell to the street on top of a sewer and died instantly.

Anthony was the first guy who Quacky shot. I had seen him around as he had gone to school with my sister, Nancy. He became crippled and confined to a wheelchair for the rest of his life.

Quacky had to go to criminal court to address the charges against him. When the judge saw the feeble-looking, eighty-year-old Quacky, he could hardly believe he had shot two people. His lawyer presented the evidence to the judge, and when the judge took notice of the black-and-blue marks on Quacky's face from the first incident, he was so angry that he fined Quacky only $2 for an unlicensed firearm.

The following week a magazine ran a story with Quacky's picture, hailing him as a vigilante hero. Some people in the neighborhood who knew how old Quacky's hidden gun was must have thought it was a wonder he'd even been able to fire it. Though the police took the gun from him, they congratulated him on winning his case. For the rest of Quacky's years in Corona he was known as "Dead-eye Jack" after a character in an old Wild West story who was a really good shot.

After Quacky came back from the lockup, everyone in the neighborhood came into his store to congratulate him. I went in with Charlie from the auto repair shop, the pharmacist from the drugstore, and several other people we knew. News reporters took photos and the next day Quacky and me was on the front page of the daily paper. I was working in construction at that time and as I rode the subway to work in Manhattan, people on the train reading the paper did double-takes and looked hard at me.

"This looks like you on the front page," a fellow commuter said.

"Yeah, it's me," I told him. "Just read the story. Everything is there."

By 1966, with two babies, Michael and Lisa, Jacqueline and me moved again, this time into a larger apartment in another building down the block from the building where I'd grown up.

One night we'd just come home from a visit at my mother-in-law's house and I left Lisa, who was just a few months old, on the kitchen table in her infant seat as Jacqueline was trying to put Michael to bed. I went to help her in the bedroom and when I came out of the bedroom to attend to Lisa, I found her on the floor crying. She must have wiggled her feet and worked her little body to the end of the kitchen table and fallen off, still in the infant seat.

I was dressed only in my pants having taken off my shoes, socks, and shirt. Jacqueline came in and started to scream. I picked Lisa up and raced, barefoot and shirtless, down the four flights of stairs to the street. The screaming in the hall brought my sister Nancy out of her first-floor apartment. I told her what had happened and that I was bringing the baby to Booth Memorial Hospital. It was chaos in the hallway of the apartment building when doors opened and people were wondering what was happening. Barefoot I made tracks on the Avenue.

My sister ran after me and grabbed Lisa, and I drove to the hospital. Jacqueline sat next to me crying her eyes out. In the emergency room with my wife and sister, I used a pay phone to call our pediatrician, Dr. Baleano, to come to the hospital. He gave me some cockamamie story about why he couldn't get there and told me that the doctors at the hospital would handle it. With that I had a few choice words for him, and I was so angry I overreacted and ripped the phone out of the wall.

The ER doctor came out and told us that everything was all right with Lisa, and thank God she didn't have any lasting effects from that fall. That was the good news; the bad news was how I'd handled the situation with nothing but anger and violence. I knew that it hadn't been the right way to handle a crisis like that, but I didn't know of a different way than the way I had always been doing. You learn in life what you are taught, and the anger I'd grown up with had become part of me.

Still, I loved my wife and children with all my heart and soul, and that was something I'd never learned from my own father. All I'd ever seen in him was wickedness and hate. Growing up, I'd spent many nights awake trying to find a way to kill him while he was sleeping. Luckily, God had a better plan for me and guided me to Jacqueline, but because of the violence and self-hatred I'd learned from Patsy, it took me years to accept her love for me. I had a lot of unlearning to do. Thank God it began to happen.

OUR WEDDING DAY

CHAPTER 13

Back in the 1960's they didn't use flash cameras to monitor the traffic as they do today. In those days the police department would set up two vehicles parked a couple hundred yards apart at the curb, your odometer would be clocked between the two cars, and that's how they determined speeding. With today's technology a traffic camera takes a photo of your license plate number and you get a citation in the mail with a letter and a copy of the photo. It's an open and shut case now, because they have proof-positive of whatever traffic violation you've committed. But that wasn't how things used to be.

One boiling hot summer afternoon I walked out of the Italian grocery store in our Queens neighborhood where I'd just bought $30 worth of cold cuts—*soppresata*, *mortadella*, cheeses—to bring to my sister-in-law's house in Nassau County. Jacqueline and the kids were already out there, and I was late to meet them so I took a road that would bring me to a shortcut to the highway.

A police officer pulled me over just before I reached the highway. When the officer approached my car, he asked me for my driver's license and registration, and at that moment, I realized I didn't have my license on me.

Growing up with Patsy had led me to a fight-or-flight response, usually to fight. But as the officer started writing the summons, I decided to take flight. I took off, speeding away from the patrol car. I didn't know where I was going; I was just driving between streets to get away. I started making as many turns as I could to try to throw off the police officer, who was now following me. The next thing I knew, I'd wound up on Main Street in Flushing. I thought I had lost him, but as I stopped for a red light on Main Street, he blocked my car with his patrol car, got out, and came over to my car.

"You're the fellow who took off when I was ready to issue you a summons for speeding."

"Officer, you have the wrong guy."

"No, I don't. I was right behind you when you fled."

I was cornered again, but this time the other response, the one more familiar to me, kicked in. I pushed the officer away from me, and he lost his balance and fell against my car. As I was trying to flee again, a second unmarked police car pulled up alongside my car, and the officer came out with his gun drawn. By then the officer I'd pushed got up, handcuffed me, and told me I was under arrest. They took me to the area precinct, where I was booked; then I was transferred to criminal court. They put me in a holding cell with about fifteen other guys.

I knew then that I was in big trouble and that it had been completely of my own making. Whenever I felt angry or threatened, I lost control of my emotions. Fighting had become my way of life.

Ray, a friend of our family worked in the courts as a jailer. His job was to move prisoners to and from arraignment in court. As he passed the holding cell that afternoon, his head jerked back for a second look and he said in surprise, "Bobby, what in hell are you doing in here?"

"Ray," I said. "I'm in big trouble."

At that moment they started to serve lunch to us in the lockup. The lunch was watered-down soup and two slices of white bread. All I could think about was that big package of cold cuts I'd left behind in my car. Suddenly, Ray came back to open up the cell and moved me to a single holding pen. I felt much more comfortable in there alone.

Three hours later Ray came to take me out of the holding cell and brought me to the court area where I was to be arraigned. I went before the judge, who started reading the long list of charges against me. The officer I'd pushed had decided to throw the book at me. He'd filed charges against me for assault on a police officer, speeding, failure to comply with an order, driving without a license, and not wearing corrective lenses.

The judge gave me a date when I had to return for trial, and then he released me on my own recognizance. I had to go down to the city impound lot and pay $90 to get my car. When I opened the door, the odor from those cold cuts lying in the sun all day was horrible. I'd live with the miserable smell if it meant I didn't have to deal with Jacqueline's anger when I finally got to her sister's house, many hours late with no phone call. She was as angry as she'd ever been with me since I'd known her.

I was arrested in June and my court date was in August. When the court date arrived, I dressed up in a nice suit. As I entered the courthouse, I was told by a court officer that I had to go to the court clerk first to obtain my file, which contained all my charges. When I approached the court clerk's window, the clerk asked, "Are you represented by counsel?"

"Naw, I'm not."

"Then I can't give you your file because you must be represented by an attorney."

"I can't afford an attorney."

At that time my construction union was on strike. I was out of work and didn't have two nickels to rub together.

"Please," I asked the clerk, "Just give me my file and I'll represent myself."

"You know it's very unusual that someone with so many charges would come to court without an attorney. You are charged with two felonies. Do you realize that if you lose this case, you'll probably be ruined for life? You won't be able to get a government or a city job. I'm just trying to help you," the clerk said. "You don't look like you've had experience with the criminal justice system."

"I haven't. I'll have to take my chances."

So there I was, dressed up in my suit, and when I entered the courtroom I immediately felt more scared and out of place than I'd ever been in my life. Nobody was defending me against the massive charges I faced. I sat at the table for the defense and a few feet away from me was the prosecutor who was representing the people. In other seats I saw police officers.

The judge in a black robe asked me, "Mr. Lauri, are you represented by an attorney?"

"No I'm not, Your Honor. I'm representing myself."

As soon as I'd said it, I remembered the old saying, "A client who represents himself has a fool for a lawyer."

"Are you sure you want to proceed with this trial today?" the judge asked.

"Yes, Your Honor."

"I want to inform you that whatever happens here, at the end of this trial you will be held accountable for your actions. Do you understand what I am conveying to you?"

"Yes, Your Honor. I'm ready to proceed with the case."

"Please call your first witness, Mr. Lauri," the judge instructed.

I called the first police officer. "How did you know that it was me you were issuing the summons to? And how did you find me, as you said I left the scene when you were going to issue me a speeding ticket?"

"You sped off and I chased after you for many blocks."

"At this time, Officer, can you produce any evidence that proves that I was the assailant who took flight?"

"I chased you through the streets of that neighborhood."

"When I looked in my rearview mirror, I didn't see anybody following me. You didn't have my license plate number. How did you know you had the right car? Did you remember the color of my car? Will you please tell the court the color of my car?"

The officer looked puzzled. He shook his head no. He couldn't answer.

"I was driving an aquamarine 1963 Pontiac Catalina."

The judge interrupted. "Sir, do you have any other questions to ask this officer?"

"No, Your Honor, no more questions."

With that, the prosecutor called me to the witness stand and he started to put questions to me to try to confuse me.

"When you took flight, was the officer behind you?"

"I didn't take flight. I got into my car and drove away, and when I drove away, the officer was just entering his car."

The judge looked upset. I thought he was probably saying to himself, *This case isn't going anywhere; there's no proof, there's no evidence, not even a license plate number.*

"Have you any more questions for this gentleman?" he asked the prosecutor.

"No, Your Honor. The people rest." The prosecutor didn't look happy.

The judge looked at me. "Does the defense rest?"

"Yes, Your Honor."

We both sat down, me at one side of the courtroom, and the police officers next to the prosecutor at another table. When the judge called a recess, I went into the hall. I was nervous and I paced as I waited for the judge to return with the verdict. After half an hour the judge returned to the courtroom. The court officer came out to the hallway to call me in. I went to my defense table and sat down alone.

The judge asked me to stand as he read all of the charges against me: assaulting a police officer, speeding, failure to comply with an order, driving without a license, and not wearing corrective lenses. As the judge read each charge, he started to dismiss them, one charge at a time. First, he dismissed the assault charge, then the speeding ticket, then the others. When he'd dismissed them all, he said, "Mr. Lauri, I am fining you $25 for court costs." He pounded his gavel. It was over. The two police officers left the courtroom quickly shaking their heads and talking quietly to each other, probably trying to figure out how I'd defended this case by myself and won. I walked over to the court clerk to pay my fine, and he looked at me in amazement.

He was shocked. "With all those charges against you, you only got a $25 fine."

I paid the fine.

"Listen, fella," the court clerk said, "The next time you get a traffic ticket you fight the ticket in traffic court and stay away from criminal court. You're a very lucky guy to beat this rap."

I smiled. "I agree. I plan on never seeing you again.

Maybe it was luck that kept me out of trouble in criminal court, or maybe it was my "lawyering" skills; but my increasingly uncontrollable temper didn't let me stay out of trouble. One morning in 1965 I was on my way to take the subway to go to work in "the City," which is how every New Yorker who doesn't actually live in Manhattan refers to that borough. I always stopped to get a newspaper, and since my station, Main Street, was the first stop on that subway line, it was always crowded in the morning with people. That morning was no exception. Approaching the entrance to the track, I could see crowds of people waiting to board the train to work.

Upon boarding, everyone scrambled to get a seat because it's at least a half-hour ride to the City. I managed to get the last seat in the last car. As I was opening up my paper to start to read the news of the day, a middle-aged man came in and pushed me off the seat trying to squeeze in next to me. It was 6:30 a.m. I was barely awake and hadn't had any coffee yet, and the rudeness of this man made me angry enough to hit him square in the face. He went down like a ton of bricks. Blood dripped from his mouth. I saw his teeth the moment before they flew out of his mouth. The poor guy was wearing false teeth.

The other passengers around us quickly scattered as much as possible in the crowded subway car. A conductor approached and said that he was stopping the train in the station. A police officer arrived on the scene and started to investigate what had taken place. First he questioned the man I'd hit and then me.

"I was sitting down reading my paper on my way to work," I told the officer, "when this man tried to squeeze into my seat. He pushed me right off the seat and I stumbled onto the floor of the train."
The officer was looking at me strangely as I gave my account until finally he asked me, "Is your name Bobby Lauri?"

"Yeah."

"Don't you remember me? It's been a long time since we've run into each other. We went to high school together."

I took a closer look and recognized him. "This is really embarrassing."

"Bobby," he said, lowering his voice, "This man wants me to arrest you, and I'd feel real bad doing that because I know you."

But he had to, and as he handcuffed me, he said, "The man said you broke his dental plate by punching him in the mouth and he wants you to pay for his damages."

He escorted me from the subway station and into his police car, and I was informed that we were going to the local precinct. At the precinct I was put in the holding pen waiting to be taken to criminal court for arraignment.

After the arraignment the criminal court judge released me without bail and instructed me to appear at a later date. Before I left the precinct, I asked the sergeant if he would be so kind as to fill out a cross-complaint against the man who had me arrested. This would put both of us on more equal legal ground. Besides, I hadn't hit him unprovoked—he had shoved me out of my seat first.

Several months later my court date came. Once again, I dressed in my good suit. I felt like I was donning a coat of armor for battle. This was the second time I was going to defend myself from an assault charge. The man I hit was sitting next to his attorney in the courtroom, but I was once again alone at the defense table to address the charges of assault and bodily harm to another person.

The man's attorney called me up to the stand and started to question me. "Why did you assault my client? All he wanted to do was sit down next to you."

"Sir, he wasn't just trying to sit down next to me. He entered the subway car like a bull in a china shop and deliberately pushed me off the seat that I was occupying onto the floor."

His attorney denied this and continued questioning me.

When he was finished, it was my turn to cross-examine the man from the train. After the judge asked him to take the witness stand, I began my questioning.

"Why were you trying to sit in a seat where there clearly wasn't enough room to sit down? You were so aggressive that I was frightened. You made a menacing gesture at me and in order to protect myself I lashed out at you."

"There was plenty of room to sit but you just got angry and hit me for no apparent reason, and you broke my dental plate."

"Sir, I'm terribly sorry that this incident took place, but I feared for my life and I had to protect myself."

When the cross-examinations were finished, the judge didn't recess the court. Instead he announced a quick decision. "I find in the action of the accused there was no criminal intent. I dismiss the entire complaint."

For the second time in my life the bang of the gavel brought a huge wave of relief, and I realized that "someone upstairs" must have really been looking out for me. I didn't know if I'd ever be that lucky again in a similar situation, so right then and there, I decided that I'd had enough of the law and the courts. I never got in trouble after that. I knew I had to learn to control my anger before it ever again brought me to the point of no return, where I might hurt someone badly enough to land me in jail for a very long time. Sitting on a seat in a jail cell gave me plenty of time to think of the big mistakes I made in life that hurt others, hurt myself, and hurt the people I love.

I decided to go for anger management counseling over the years but it wasn't until after 9/11 when I went to a psychiatrist and started taking medication that I was able to conquer it. That helped me deal with the anger issues. I'd carried the baggage of my father's abuse well into my adulthood and I was sad to think of the many good friends I'd lost along the way because of my anger. Through counseling I learned to understand their reasoning, but before then everything was everyone else's fault. I'm truly sorry for all of the problems I unloaded on my friends and relatives with my actions.

After living for two years in a third-floor apartment with two small children, Jacqueline and me decided to look for a house. Every time Jacqueline went grocery shopping my godfather Charlie used to help her carry the baby carriage and the food up the three flights of stairs. After doing this for a while, my godfather told me in Italian, "*Goombah*, you've got to get yourself a house. I can't keep bringing the groceries up three flights of stairs."

One day soon after that, Charlie called me into the dress shop where he worked, and said, "*Goombah,* I am going to give you $20,000 to put down on a home."

I was dumbfounded. "I'll only take the money if your nephew Richie will make out a legal document that says I have to pay you back in a certain amount of time."

"No," Charlie shook his head. "I want you to have it as a gift"

"You worked all your life emptying freight cars full of brick and mortar bags and putting them on pallets all day long day after day. I used to see you sweat a lot in the summertime when I came to your workplace. If you don't have Richie make the loan paper out, I won't take the dough."

I was firm on that. At that point he said, "Call Richie and have him do what you want."

Richie, Charlie's nephew, was a lawyer and he was a nice guy, always smiling and laughing. I called him and he called back with the word that I should come to his office in the City to sign the papers. When I got there and met with him he said, "Before you sign, I have to tell you that when you make out a loan for a mortgage, you must put a time, date, and interest percentage on the paper. Charlie wants to give you the money without interest. His terms are for you to just send a monthly payment with whatever amount you want."

"That's great!" I said and I signed the note.

CHAPTER 14

That night in the living room when Jacqueline and me were sitting on the sofa, I put my arm around her shoulder. "Hon, now that we have the money I'd like to tell Patsy that we're buying a house and moving away."

"Don't tell him. It's none of his business."

I understood why she felt this way; she'd already seen and heard enough to know what he was like, and she'd stored up a great deal of anger toward him, especially from living through what his abuse had done to me.

"If we don't tell him, he'll never talk to us again."

I knew the wickedness of this man, but I tried to stay in his good graces somewhat in spite of it for the sake of the relationship with the rest of my family. We decided to tell him when we were visiting my sister in her apartment on the first floor. Nancy, her husband, and Patsy were there.

I said, "My wife and me are going to buy a house in Flushing. Charlie has lent us money."

You shoulda seen the look on his face. If looks could kill, both Jacqueline and me would be dead.

"Why are you movin'?"

"Charlie and me can't carry so many heavy things up the stairs no more. Plus, I have a boy and a girl. I'd like them to have their own bedrooms."

At that point he had a mean look as he said something evil-sounding, "I'd kill one instead." You would've needed to be there to believe it. He was charming and very friendly to strangers and he treated my sisters well as long as they did whatever he asked, but he always had a negative or sarcastic remark where I was concerned. Who would say such a terrible thing about a grandchild? What was also terrible was that when I looked in the mirror, I saw him. I have his face. He looked like an ordinary man, medium height, dark hair and dark eyes. You'd never think looking at him that he was born without a heart.

We bought the house, just one town away. When we moved in, of course, Patsy didn't come to wish us luck. He also kept my sisters from coming to my house for three years. He always tried to keep us apart and they were afraid of him. He threatened to disinherit them if they didn't listen to him. He wanted total control over his family; it was either his way or the highway. He often told me, "I'm leaving you a dollar so you can buy a rope and hang yourself."

I answered, whenever he said that, "I'll paste that dollar to your forehead in the coffin."

He loved using his last will and testament to control us, but I didn't give a crap about it. The most galling thing about it was that he barely owned the clothes on his back outright. My mother's father Michael owned three buildings in Corona, and before he died, he put Patsy's name with my mother's on the two six-family houses. He then gave the dilapidated two-family house to Patsy alone in his name, with the condition that he leave his nephew, Joey, a thousand dollars. My grandfather passed away in 1950. Without the property Patsy wouldn't have had any financial security.

After about four years of marriage, unfortunately, I started to exhibit Patsy's family ways. I yelled at my wife and at Michael and Lisa. I became violent with strangers and argumentative at home, and I didn't realize I was becoming like my father. There were times when Jacqueline would go to bed crying over some disagreement we had that night. I would lie next to her without saying a word even though I heard her crying.

One day Michael stayed out all day playing with friends and he came home at about nine o'clock at night. I was so angry with him that I threw a stick at him. It hit him in the face. I can imagine how much he must have hated me. In later years, as time passed, I knew he hadn't forgotten about it because from time to time he repeated the story.

Every time I said, "Michael, I'm so sorry for what I did. I hope someday you'll forgive me."

I was once talking to a neighbor who had seen me walking around on crutches and had asked what had happened to me. I had to tell him that trying to prove a point had cost me twenty-six stitches between my toes. I'd gone outside and found my daughter Lisa and her cousin jumping on my car. After yelling at them, I went back inside where another neighbor was visiting with Jacqueline. I was fuming and trying to explain to the neighbor that this wasn't a normal thing for kids to do.

"Sure it is," the neighbor replied casually.

That made me so angry that I got off my chair and started jumping on the kitchen table to show how abnormal it was to jump on things. The next thing I knew the table collapsed and I fell to the floor. My poor wife was in shock. When I took off my sock, I was bleeding a lot. I wrapped a towel around my foot. Jacqueline drove me to the hospital where I received twenty-six stitches and a pair of crutches. That was how it was then. My emotional outbursts damaged others as well as me.

Another time we were having a birthday party for Lisa in our backyard with friends and family and we were all having a great time. Suddenly, Lisa ran into the backyard bleeding from her front tooth. She had been riding her bike when she hit a tree and flew off her bike, slamming her face on the concrete.

Again, knowing no other way to handle the situation, I threw the bike down the flight of stairs into the basement. Everyone looked at me as if I had been a maniac, and rightfully so. Thankfully, my sister Susan held and comforted Lisa, who was screaming and crying because she was in so much pain.

My angry outbursts were unnerving and often downright frightening to those around me, but sometimes they resulted in a little humor at my expense. When the holidays came one year, I bought a Christmas tree and put it in our dining room. The room was nearly empty because we hadn't yet bought a dining room set, so it was the best place to put the tree. We decorated the tree with lights, Christmas balls, and tinsel and it looked beautiful. There was only one problem. The tree would not stay in place. It kept falling over, so I tried to tie it to the wall behind it. It still would not stay up. It started to get to me.

A few friends stopped over one night to wish me and my family a merry Christmas. Pete one of my friends, was watching me try to get the tree to stand up straight. I was getting angry. Here we go again. I am what I was taught. I started to punch the tree all around the dining room. As usual everybody was looking at me like I was some kind of nut. With that, I picked up the tree, lights and all, and threw it out on the front lawn.

Pete stood up and said, "Bobby, I'm going home."

As he was leaving, he picked up the tree on my front lawn, put it in his car and took it home. The next time I saw Pete he told me that when he brought the tree into his house, his wife asked him, "Since when do you buy a Christmas tree all decorated with lights and bulbs?"

He told her it was a long story and he would tell her another time. Then, he told me that it was the best tree he ever had in his life. We got a big laugh about it.

* * *

People used to ask me what being successful in life feels like.

"It's when your alarm clock is ringing and you can shut it off. You turn over and go back to sleep. That's when you've made a success out of your life."

Don't talk about success as just having leisure time in retirement. I'm talking about working from a very young age as I did, from as young as seven years old until I retired at the age of sixty-one. Success is when you can retire and not have to worry about getting another job to make ends meet.

In today's world, some people have to work way past retirement age, some until they drop dead on the job and they're carried out on a stretcher. It's not how much dough we earn during our working years; it's how we save for the future, achieve goals, and look back on a life well-lived. It's learning from mistakes and teaching the younger generation not to make the same mistakes we did.

As a kid growing up, I knew how it felt to be poor, and then I also knew how it felt to be broke most of my married life. Everything in those years was a financial drain; no matter how much money I made, it was never enough. When our kids were small and the ice cream truck drove down our street, my poor wife didn't even have enough money to buy them ice cream.

Things started to get better as my life went on. I worked in the thermostat field for about seven years. I had a house that had two mortgages on it and all the money for buying the house was borrowed. I hadn't put one cent down on that house and I didn't care. All I knew was that I had a beautiful home for my family. I couldn't care less how I would pay for the house, as long as I had gotten out of the apartment in Corona and away from people who didn't care about us.

Patsy had a huge influence over my two sisters and their husbands. I remember visiting my sister's apartment and watching television. Patsy came into the living room, went over and changed the channel, and nobody said a word. We all kept quiet. He had no respect for no one in the family.

At least, I don't say the same about his sisters and brothers. I loved my Aunt Louise, who was always smiling, and my Uncle Arnie. Growing up, I spent most of my summers at Uncle Arnie's and Aunt Phyllis' home in East Islip on Long Island. Uncle Arnie used to take us kids to the bakery on Carlton Avenue in the mornings for the warmest buns you could find. Their children, my cousins, were Arnie and Maria. My poor cousin Arnie passed away young—he was only forty-eight when he died. I loved him dearly, and my summer months with his family are full of memories that I'll always cherish. At night when we went to bed, my Aunt Phyllis came up to our bedrooms and gave a blessing to Arnie, then she went into Maria's room and did the same thing, and then she came into my room and blessed me. All of my aunts and uncles were aware of the miserable life I had growing up with Patsy, and they were all very compassionate towards me.

My Aunt Antoinette was a great baker and my cousin Toni, her daughter, and me hung out a lot. Uncle Tom was Aunt Antoinette's husband and he picked me up on his knee and tickled my belly until I laughed my head off. I never got to know much about my Aunt Fanny because she passed away when I was very young. Uncle Benny was single and never married. He wasn't a happy man and hardly ever smiled, but the one thing that made him happy was a pack of cigarettes. Aunt Florie had been exiled from the Lauri family before I was born and I never found out why. It was something that Patsy and my aunts and uncles never discussed around us kids.

The families on my wife's side were the greatest people you'd ever want to know. There have always been mother-in-law jokes, but none of them applied to my mother-in-law Nancy. I truly loved her and everyone else. She had three sisters, Pauline, Mary, and Jean. Aunt Pauline was married to Uncle Bob, Aunt Mary was married to Uncle Joe, and Aunt Jean was married to Uncle Mike. They also had a brother named Michael, who was married to Aunt Lillian. They were a loving and close-knit family, completely unlike my own.

Jacqueline, me, and the kids would go on a Sunday to eat at Aunt Mary's and Uncle Joe's. How I remember Uncle Joe and Aunt Mary's outstanding meat sauce. Uncle Joe stood at the sauce pot for an hour stirring the garlic and tomato paste—slowly, over and over, until the mixture was dark. Then he and Aunt Mary switched places and she did the same. You never tasted a sauce like that in your life. We sat around the table and ate all day and besides, having good-natured battles over the current events of the week, we talked about horses and boxing. The following week at Aunt Jean's and Uncle Mike's house the conversation was about tennis and baseball.

Uncle Mike was a chair referee on the United States Tennis Association (USTA) courts in what is now Arthur Ashe Stadium and the Forest Hills Stadium. He used to referee professional tennis matches. He was the kindest, gentlest man you could talk to and I wished with all my heart that he'd been my father.

Not one of my wife's aunts and uncles ever spoke an angry word to me or about me. I'd never experienced love like that at home as a child or as an adult, but I received that love and was embraced by my wife's aunts and uncles and I felt they were mine. I had wanted that so much in my life. Now, years later, I regret not spending more time with them and their families. They helped me realize that my life was like a flowering plant. In order to bring it to its fullest promise and most beautiful bloom, with its brightest colors, you had to nurture it with care by watering it and feeding it with plant food and making sure that it had the proper light. Then you saw the vibrant results of your nurturing care.

It's the same thing when you are raising a child. If you don't nurture the child with love and care, the child will grow up with a poor state of mind. If you beat the child for everything that happens in the course of the day, you create a twisted, violent piece of humanity. But if you handle the child with kindness, love, and respect, he'll return the same to you. He'll not continue the brutality of the hand or strap, not having experienced them.

* * *

In 1969 two of my closest friends and me decided to take a trip to Las Vegas. Frank Lorfrice, my neighbor Frank Mistara, and me were in Vegas for eight days. It felt like a lifetime. We stayed at the Aladdin Hotel and from there we branched out to different casinos. We went to The Sands, The Dunes, and The Stardust Hotel. We went to every hotel up and down the Strip.

The first night we were in Vegas I stopped in at the Sands Hotel, where Louie Prima was appearing on stage. I thought of him as "the one and only" greatest entertainer in show business. Sam Butera and the Witnesses were playing.

When I was about fifteen years old, I had listened to Louie Prima and Keely Smith on the Capital label—live from both the Sands Hotel and the Sahara Hotel. He was my idol.

ME AND SAM BUTERA

Every night in Vegas my friends and me got dressed to the nines and went out on the town. I always wound up going to see Louie and Sam at the Sands. For three shows a night—every night over eight days—I sat at the front table, ordered my drinks, and forgot why I went to Las Vegas in the first place. On the last night, at the last show, a *maître d'* handed me a note that changed my life. As he placed the note in my hand, he whispered in my ear, "Mr. Prima wants to see you in his dressing room."

Boy did I feel good. A couple of Stingers helped. I went backstage and found the dressing room. There was a star on the door, which read *Louie Prima*. I knocked on the door. Mr. Prima wearing a smart-looking robe motioned me to come in. "Have a seat," he said. "I noticed you sitting at the front table watching my show every night for a week, three shows a night at 9:00 p.m., midnight, and 3:00 a.m. For what reason?"

"I went to all your shows because you're one of my favorite entertainers, along with Frank Sinatra. I used to have a little band back east when I was playing jobs for $5.00 once a month on a Friday night at the VFW. I sang all your songs with the shuffle beat to tunes like 'Hey Marie,'

104

'When You're Smiling,' and many of the great hits you had on Capital Records. I even remember you on the Dot label."

"Is that so? How would you like to be my road manager back east, also with Sam Butera's band?"

Sam Butera and the Witnesses had been Louie Prima's band for years, practically since Louie's first gig in Vegas. Louie hated to fly, so he planned to travel around on tour in a thirty-foot motor home with a driver. I didn't understand at first what he meant about going out on the road.

"Mr. Prima, I don't understand. Isn't Vegas your hometown?"

"No. I've spent many years performing in Vegas at all the big venues: the Sahara, the Hilton, the Sands, and the Riviera. Las Vegas is ending its lounge shows for entertainers—not only for him, but for other noted musicians, such as Matt Monroe, Mat Dennis, and Buddy Greco. I'm going back east to tour clubs in the tri-state area—New York, New Jersey, and Connecticut."

I did not hesitate one second before I said, "Yeah, I'll take the job. Thanks a lot."

LOUIS PRIMA AND ME

CHAPTER 15

As I'd hoped, when I got home and told Jacqueline about this opportunity, she was very happy and excited for me, even though it meant I'd be away from her and the kids. Having been in the music business, I knew what it was to be a road-manager. You and the band mostly live in hotels or motels. A road manager or tour manager has to make sure the band knows what time they go onstage. He has to work with the theater manager on sound checking the microphones and equipment and setting all the microphones at a specific level. As Louie Prima's road manager, I would have to wake up all the boys in the band the morning after a gig to get moving again. Getting six guys to leave at one time was nearly impossible.

Later I learned that the piano player wanted to sleep a little longer, the trumpet player complained that we were leaving too early, but, finally, I was able to get everybody on board. In the motor home was me, Louie, and Rolly Dee, the bass player. Sam rode with the boys as he didn't like riding in the motor home to make it to the next job.

It was wonderful that the jobs did materialize. Rolly Dee became my partner, and we loaded up the motor home with enough water and food to take everyone to the next gig, maybe three or four hours' drive away.

Louie Prima was always called "The Chief." I never called him by his name, but I always was by his side or within view of wherever he was. He liked to exercise while on tour by walking around the parking area of wherever we were and I had to keep an eye on him. When people eventually noticed he was there, they always asked for an autograph. It was my job to ask them to please let him finish his walking first.

My first time working for Louie Prima and his band on tour was in 1970. I still had a good paying job installing thermostats and climate control systems; I didn't need the money, so I told "The Chief," my heartfelt truth: that it was an honor for me to be his road manager. Spending time with a very great entertainer was a dream come true.

I met most of the band members at Kennedy Airport. Rolly D'Orio drove "The Chief" in the motor home. The first Long Island booking was a week at the Westbury Music Fair. The place was packed every night with two shows a night.

After that week the band headed to Philadelphia, where Louie was booked at Palumbo's off of the Ninth Street Italian Market. Rolly drove the motor home, I sat next to him in the passenger seat, and Louie slept in back. Near the Walt Whitman Bridge Rolly said he was tired driving, so he asked me to take over. I told him I had never driven a motor home this large; it was as big as a tractor-trailer. Rolly assured me—perhaps foolishly—that I would be fine. We switched seats right after the bridge. Rolly told me to remember to make a right turn on Ninth Street.

When I got to Ninth Street and made the turn, I noticed that the Italian Market was just closing and the street was loaded with garbage and boxes waiting for the sanitation truck to pick them up. Rolly saw the packed street and started to curse in Italian. I could not back up at that point and had to proceed very slowly down the block scraping boxes and garbage on either side of the vehicle. We finally got through, Louie never heard a sound, and all was well with the motor home. Rolly and I were quite relieved, as you can imagine.

I was thirty-two and I'd been Louie Prima's road manager for a couple of years, whenever he toured in the tri-state area. He'd come back east and tour for a few months a year and I'd join them. I loved those road trips.

When "The Chief" was traveling around the New York area on tour, he came back to Long Island at night and stayed at the Island Inn in Garden City. I went back home, about fifteen miles away, during the day and came back at night in time to work with the stagehands and do the sound checks. There were always celebrities coming backstage both to greet Louie and to work with him. One week Peter Lemongello opened up for him. Popular stand-up comedian Marty Allen came in one night, and another time singer/actress Toni Arden stopped by.

The day after one of the Long Island shows Louie and Rolly had a golf date. I drove Louie, Rolly, and my brother-in-law, Sally, to the country club. As a joke the guys who we played with gave Louie a gift of a golf club that looked like a hammer. We all laughed, watching Louie take a couple of swings with it. Then, "The Chief" teed off and the ball hooked to the right, so he told me to get another ball. I got it from Rolly. After Louie's next ball hooked to the left, I had to get yet another ball from Rolly. He was not a "happy camper" about this as each ball cost three dollars—rather expensive for a golf ball in those days.

ME AND THE HAMMER HEAD GOLF CLUB

When we finished playing golf, we headed for the show with a stop for dinner at the Sans Souci Club. I didn't have directions. There was no such thing as a GPS or cell phones back then, so I made telephone calls. My brother-in-law Sally, who was with me, suggested I try to get Louie to go to Mickey Allen's Supper Club in Lawrence, Long Island, instead. I told him we had been planning to meet the owner of the Sans Souci club for dinner. When I got back in the car and started to drive, I mentioned to Louie that I had a cousin who owned a restaurant and that the food there was very good. Louie was quiet for a long while and finally agreed that we could go to my cousin's restaurant. My cousin Chubby was there along with Mickey Allen. They were thrilled we came there and prepared a table for us.

Vincenzo, the chef excitedly came out to greet Louie and ask what special meal he could make for him. Louie wanted *cannelloni*, which are large pasta tubes filled with meat and vegetables, similar to *manicotti*. Vincenzo said he felt like a little boy back in Italy meeting his hero when he brought out the food. We all had dinner and took some pictures and then we left to go back to the hotel so Louie could get ready for that night's show.

The night before the show closed at Westbury Louie spoke to me in the dressing room, "Bobby, tomorrow night I want to give a tribute and make an appearance at your cousin's restaurant. Tell the boys that after the show we're all going to Mickey Allen's Supper Club and have some fun."

Nobody else was supposed to know that Louie Prima and Sam Butera and the Witnesses were going to appear at the club, but somehow the local paper got tipped off. The place was packed wall-to-wall with people. There wasn't a single empty seat. Louie didn't stay long, but Sam and the boys played until three in the morning. It felt like being at a Vegas lounge instead of a little club on Long Island.

The following year Louie and the band came to Westbury again—with the comedian Pat Cooper and Napoli & Glasson opening. After the week at Westbury we had to head up to Connecticut to do a couple of shows. After the last Westbury show the boys in the band told Louie they were very hungry. "Bobby," he said, "Where can we get some meatball sandwiches?" It was eleven-thirty at night and we had a long ride to Connecticut ahead. I knew of a nearby place called Mario's Restaurant, so

I called and asked the owner if it would be possible for him to make a dozen meatball hero sandwiches. Mario said they were just closing up for the night and he wished I'd called him a little earlier.

PAT COOPER AND ME

"Listen, my name is Bob Lauri and I'm the road manager for Louie Prima and Sam Butera. We just got finished playing at Westbury, we're heading out of state, and I need you to make some meatball sandwiches for us to take on the road with us. I'm terribly sorry about the short notice, but we're starved. I'm just leaving the theater now and can be at your place in about forty-five minutes."

Within an hour we were enjoying delicious meatball sandwiches.

Louie, Rolly, and me were in the motor home and the boys followed us in a big van. We arrived late at the Howard Johnson's Hotel in Connecticut. We all had breakfast in the morning, and some of Louie's friends had set up a round of golf right afterward. We met up with friends in the hotel lobby and we were getting ready to leave when Jack asked me if I'd mind not joining them for golf.

"That's great!" I said. "Now I can go back and get some much-needed rest."

As they were getting into the van provided by the hotel, Louie asked Jack where I was. Jack said that he'd asked me if I wouldn't mind staying back for today.

"Go call Bobby," Louie said. When I came down from my room, Louie told Jack, "Bobby comes with me."

I saw the look of embarrassment on Jack's face. He apologized to me and I told him it was no big deal. Jack let it go. I thought to myself: *I knew Louie would not go without me, but hey, you tried. I would have loved the day off.*

Before the show that night I did the sound check with the band. As the band started to play the first song, the lights went out in the whole place and all that came on were the emergency lights. People went outside and they noticed that the pole that carried the electric wires into the club was burning on top, causing the blackout. As they waited to see what the owners were going to do, I noticed "the one and only Joe DiMaggio" sitting at a table.

I thought, *Boy would I like to get an autograph from him for my son.* Joe DiMaggio, however, did not regularly sign autographs. When I approached him and tried to get him to notice me, it seemed like he was ignoring me since he would not turn around. Then I said to him, "Mr. DiMaggio, my name is Bobby Lauri and I am with the Louie Prima show." With that he gave me the biggest smile you can imagine and took a pen out of his pocket and asked, "Do you have anything for me to write on?" I handed him a little notepad and he got ready to sign an autograph for my son. "What's your son's name?" he asked.

"Michael." I practically jumped for joy.

The lights still hadn't come back on and the owner of the club came over to me and instructed me to tell Mr. Prima to go on and do his show. So the show went on without the electricity needed for the band.

The following night Louie played at Theater in the Round in Wallingford, Connecticut. Sergio Franchi opened the show. Sergio sang beautifully that night. I remembered another tour we'd done with him when the guys in Louie's band wanted to open a couple of bottles of wine but didn't have a wine opener. Sergio's room was right next to mine, so I knocked on his door. When he opened the door, I said, "Serge, do you have a wine opener you could lend me?"

"Sure," he said, "Hold on, I'll get it for you."

When I went to return the wine opener the next day, he said to me, "Bobby, keep it."

To this day I still have and cherish that wine opener. Sergio Franchi was one great guy and I loved being around him.

CHAPTER 16

I was thirty in June and Louie was back on Long Island, with me as his East Coast road manager. We were scheduled to play Westbury. At the end of the first night's show we went to the motor home and Rolly drove us back to the Island Inn where my car was parked.

The next morning I went back to the Island Inn to meet "The Chief," but I couldn't find him so I went to the front desk clerk. "Do you know where Mr. Louie Prima is?"

"Sorry sir, but he checked out."

"Where did he go to?"

"Sorry, I don't know."

I called Rolly's room. "Where's Louie?"

"Louie went across the street to the Holiday Inn. He decided to change hotels because his wife Gia and his kids, Louis, Jr. and Lena Anne are coming in from Las Vegas for the week."

(When they grew up, Louis, Jr., started his own band. He plays excellent trumpet, just like his Dad. Lena Ann sings like her mother Gia who sang in Louie's band. When she joined, she didn't have to audition for the job, she knew every arrangement that Louie did and she fit right in, so it meant less work and rehearsal time for Louie. To this day Louis, Jr., and Lena Anne sometimes work together in Atlantic City and Las Vegas. They perform some of their parents' much-loved routines.)

When I went across the street to meet up with Louie, he was bustling around his new, larger suite, moving furniture around to make it look as comfortable as possible for his family.

"Please, Bobby and Rolly, will you pick up my wife and kids at the airport?" Louie was always concerned about the welfare of his family.

Rolly drove the motor home and I was his navigator in the passenger seat. We picked up Gia and the children and drove them back to the Holiday Inn to meet Louie. They were coming to see him perform at Westbury that night.

After the show Louie and me were in his dressing room. Louie said, "Can you help me out by finding something fun to do with my kids tomorrow?"

"How about an amusement park?"

Then Louie had a suggestion that pleased me. "Maybe you and your kids could come along with us and we'll all have a good time."

The next day my daughter Lisa and me met Louie and his family at the hotel and I drove everyone to Adventureland in Farmingdale.

When we got to the park, Louie asked me to get some tickets for the rides. I went over to the ticket window and handed the clerk $50.

"How many tickets do you want?" the clerk asked. He looked up and noticed Louie and the kids waiting.

"Is that Louie Prima?" he asked.

"It sure is."

He handed me a stack of tickets worth $100. "Have a great time on me," he said.

A highlight of the day was seeing Louie on a train ride with our kids. He was having as good a time as they were.

After rides in the Bumper Cars, going on the Ferris Wheel, and the Merry-Go-Round, and many other rides we were exhausted. It had been a long wonderful day at the park. We had smelled the popcorn, hot dogs, and French fries, but we didn't eat the junk food. The smells were driving us bananas. We were all starving for dinner.

Louie said, "Do you think we can eat at your cousin's restaurant?"

"Mickey Allen's restaurant is closed. No one knows where Vincenzo, the chef is working.

"Find out," Louie said. "I'm craving his food."

We all piled into my car and started out on the road to find Vincenzo.

In those days there was no Internet and no cell phones. Every time you had to make a call you had to stop the car and get out to find a pay phone. When I found a phone, I called my brother-in-law Sally.

"Hi, Sal, do you know where Vincenzo is working?"

"Somewhere in Hicksville. He owns his own restaurant. But I don't know the name or where it is."

Louie had me driving around the area for over an hour and the kids were getting hungry and uneasy. Gia was starting to get aggravated with Louie. Even I was a little upset after over an hour of driving up and down Route 106.

I stopped at Sears and got out of the car. There was a man in the parking lot who had just come out of the department store. I asked him, "Do you happen to know of an Italian restaurant in the area under the name of Vincenzo?"

I was lucky. The man said, "Sure, Vincenzo's is right next door."

I got back in my car and told "The Chief," "You aren't going to believe this, but Vincenzo's is right next to Sears."

Louie broke out in a smile from ear to ear. After we parked the car and entered the restaurant, Chef Vincenzo walked out of the kitchen wearing his big chef's hat. He greeted us delightedly, and I told him I had been driving a long time because Louie would not go to any other restaurant and we simply had to find his place.

He smiled and hugged Louie. Louie said to Vincenzo, "I love your *cannelloni*. Please make it for me."

Vincenzo grinned. "I make it just like the first time ya ate it."

We all ate like the starved people we were. After dinner Louie got up to applaud the chef. Louie was the happiest man in the world. He had gotten what he longed for.

We then dropped Gia and her kids off at the hotel to get dressed for the show that night. I was going to take Lisa home and come back to work the show, when Louie and Gia asked if Lisa could go to the hotel pool with their kids.

"Yeah, why not," I said.

They all had the time of their lives.

The next day Louie and his whole family headed up to Purchase, New York, where Louie was going to perform at a private party for Charlie Yellen. There was a beautiful pool on the estate and later that afternoon Gia, her kids, and me went down to the pool to have some fun in the water.

I sat with Gia beside the pool watching her kids play when Gia said, "I really didn't know much about you, Bobby, but I see how much my husband loves you. He trusts you very much."

"That makes me happy," I said.

"Louie has never really gotten close to anyone. The only other person he has felt close to besides you," she told me, "has been his mother Angelina."

"Thanks. That's the best compliment anyone has ever given me."

Gia and the kids flew back to Las Vegas after that show while Louie and the band and me traveled to Rockland County, New York, to do a show at the Nanuet Theatre-Go-Round. On the bill with Louie were The Golddiggers, who were regulars on Dean Martin's TV show, and Mickey Marvin, a comedian.

When we arrived at the theater, Louie went to his dressing room, and I went to the stage to check the sound and the placement of the mikes. Before the show started, one of the owners came over to me and said, "Louie Prima is looking for you."

I went back to Louie's dressing room. He said, "Get me some Tylenol." He looked sick and it looked like he was in a lot of pain. I got him the Tylenol bottle and put two pills in his hand.

"Give me six," he said.

"Six are too many."

"I have a brutal headache."

In spite of his headache Louie did a fantastic show that night. I couldn't believe my eyes as I watched him perform at his very best. You would never know he had such a bad headache. The crowd loved him. As always, he told Sam and the boys, "Play pretty for the people."

After Nanuet Louie and the band were supposed to go to Valley Forge, Pennsylvania, but instead, Louie went home to Las Vegas. I was told by Sam Butera that Louie had then gone to Cedars Sinai Medical Center in Los Angeles for an MRI (Magnetic Resonance Imaging). He had been diagnosed with a tumor on his brain stem and given a ten-percent chance of survival.

He had an operation to shave the tumor down, but Louie went into a coma during surgery, and he never awoke from it. He was then moved to , in New Orleans, where he originally came from. I was devastated.

I read in the newspaper, "Song stylist, Mr. Louie Prima, known for his vocal renditions of 'Che la Luna' and 'Angelina,' among other classics, has passed away." Louie had been hospitalized in a coma at Ochsner Foundation Hospital in New Orleans, Louisiana, for three years. My heart sank as my eyes teared up. Louie had been one of the best people in my life.

CHAPTER 17

After Louie Prima passed away to my sorrow, I didn't hear from anyone in the business for a while.

Sam Butera, Louie's celebrated sax player and co-composer, was the leader of Louie's backup band, The Witnesses. Sam had played for years in New Orleans at many of Bourbon Street's hottest venues, including Preservation Hall and The Famous Door. He also played at a club called The 500 Club that was owned by Louie Prima's brother Leon.

When Louie first booked his run at the Sahara in Las Vegas in December 1956, he had no backup band and quickly got hold of Sam by phone, asking him to scrape up a group and bring it out to Vegas immediately. Louie wanted him to make the trip that night, but Sam told him, "Louie, it's Christmas and I want to be with my family."

Sam left the following day and he made that trip so quickly that he didn't even have time to come up with a name. When Louie asked him to introduce the band during their first show together, Sam came up with the name, The Witnesses, on the spot.

Sam went on to play with Louie and The Witnesses for twenty-three years. The musicians included Rolly D'Orio, Morgan Thomas, Jimmy Vincent, Bruce Zonka, and Red Blount. Once Louie was gone, Sam continued playing with the band. This became a legal issue, as the name "The Witnesses" belonged on paper to Louie's estate, because Louie had paid the musicians' salaries. Sam and the other interested parties battled over the issue for a couple of years before Sam changed the band's name to "The Wildest."

A few years after Louie's death I got a call from Sam, "Bobby, would you like to join me and the band back east on the road to do some shows?"

I liked this offer. "I'll join you with pleasure."

I still had my day job, and I could take off whenever I wanted, so I met up with the band back in the City. It was the same arrangement as when I was Louie's road manager. I never received any money except expenses for working the road trips and I was fine with that. Just being with the band was enough. I realized how much I missed that exciting part of my life.

When Sam Butera started touring with his renamed band, The Wildest, they changed their entire show and began playing Top 40 music. They had Sandy Williams, who was a great female singer, but they weren't drawing crowds.

Sam and I talked at the end of every show about why they weren't more popular. When Sam played with Louie Prima, Louie gave him solos and put him in the limelight. Back in their Vegas heyday they'd shared the stage, Louie on trumpet and Sam on sax; and together they defined the music of that era.

"I wonder," Sam said to me, "How come my band and I seem to have lost our appeal? "Look, I think you have to go back to the music that made you and Louie Prima stars. Go back to Las Vegas and regroup. Form the same type of band you had with Louie. Make the music you were known for. You're not making any money to talk about now so what do you have to lose? When you think you've found what you're looking for, call me and we'll go back on the road again."

Two years later I got a call from Sam. "I'm opening up at the Rainbow Grill in Manhattan. I wanted you and Jacqueline to come as my guests to see me perform with Keely Smith, who's touring with me."

Keely Smith was a jazz and popular music singer who had performed for years with The Witnesses in Las Vegas. She'd been married to Louie, before Gia, for eight years and had a successful career in her own right.

That night when we arrived at the Rainbow Grill, we got a front-row table. Jacqueline's brother Sal and Tony Deous, a friend of his, were there. The show started and Sam opened up with his theme song "When You're Smiling." He then introduced Keely Smith and the crowd went nuts. When Keely started to sing "I Wish You Love," her signature song, she stopped suddenly, having recognized Tony Deous in the audience.

Keeley spoke to the audience, "When I was fifteen years old and living with my mother in Virginia, we were very poor." She pointed to Tony. "Tony Deous had been in the US Navy and we met at the PX at the Norfolk Naval Base. Tony saw how poor we were so one night he bought a ham and brought it to my house. My mother cooked the ham, and we all had a wonderful dinner. I never forgot that, and here he is tonight right in front of me! Please give him a very warm 'Hello' and a hearty round of applause!"

Tony stood up and thanked the audience. When he sat back down, beaming, all I could do was stare at him in disbelief. For years Tony had told that story every time we were in a bar and heard one of Louie's and Keely's hit songs on the jukebox. We never believed him because he used to kid a lot.

When the show was over, we all went backstage to Sam's dressing room. Sam turned to me and said, "What do you think of the band?"

"I'm sure glad you followed my advice and formed a band like Louie's."

He had the original shuffle beat and mastery of the songs he did with Louie and Keely when they first started at the Sahara and he was ready to take audiences by storm again.

As Sam Butera's road manager I distributed the payroll to the band and crew at the end of the week. I handled all the things that the star of the show didn't want to handle. If show times were changed, I let the band know the new schedule. If Sam asked me to look into a situation, no matter how difficult it was, I tried my utmost to settle the matter.

Sam booked gigs at Resorts International Casino Hotel in Atlantic City for twenty-four weeks out of the year. The rest of the time he played in Vegas. Sam's dressing room at Resorts International was right off the stage area. That's where he went after the show to change his clothes. I usually hung out with Sam while we waited for the next show to start.

One night after Sam's show there was a knock at the dressing room door. A handsome man and a gorgeous blonde with him came to say hello to Sam after the show. I had the guests wait outside five minutes for Sam to finish changing his clothes. When they finally came into the room, they exchanged greetings with him and told him how much they'd enjoyed the show.

I found out a little later that the man was David Hasselhoff, the star of Baywatch and Knight Rider—two very popular TV shows in the '80s. Boy was I a fool with that one! I should've let Mr. Hasselhoff and the blonde sit down inside.

When I got home after that weekend, I told Jacqueline, "I stalled a gentleman from entering the dressing room the other night. I didn't know who he was, and then I found out it was David Hasselhoff and his girlfriend."

My wife said, "How could you do such a thing! Don't you know how popular he is? He has his own show on TV called Baywatch!"

What did I know? I never had time to watch TV. "I'm sorry," I said, "I had no idea who he was. Anyway, after Sam got dressed, I let him in and all was fine."

Jacqueline just looked at me and shook her head.

One night Sam and me and a few guys were talking in his dressing room after his show. For some reason Johnny Carson's name came up. Sam said, "Louie, Keely, and I never worked The Tonight Show.

One night when I was working with Louie in the Sahara Hotel Lounge in Vegas Johnny Carson came in. When we finished the show, Carson got up on stage and started fooling around with the drums. Louie asked me, 'Who is that guy on the drums?' I told him, 'That's Johnny Carson, an up-and-coming comedian.' Louie asked me to tell him to stop playing the drums. I told him that the entertainment director didn't like anyone messing with the instruments. So I told him to stop."

Sam tapped his foot on the floor.

"That was before Johnny Carson became the host of The Tonight Show. Bobby, I guess he must've taken offense at my asking him to stop playing the drums. That may well have been the reason Louie, Keely, and I were never once booked on his show."

CHAPTER 18

I was working one weekend with Sam's show at Resorts International when I saw Sam sitting down with a couple of men I didn't know in what looked like a meeting. Sam called me over, and introduced me, "This is Bobby Lauri, my road manager."

Ezra was one of the men who I later found out was a movie director. Sam had been thinking of filming a video at Resorts International during the upcoming week. The following Thursday when I arrived back at the Seaside Hotel, across the street from Resorts International, where we always stayed when Sam was in town, I noticed a big forty-foot-long trailer at Resorts International.

When I met up with Sam, he said, "We're going to shoot the video on Friday night, around Resorts International gambling area at the boardwalk entrance of the hotel. The band will be doing a live-performance video that we'll finish on Saturday night. It'll be completed on Sunday night."

All was going well and on Sunday morning before I left Atlantic City for home Sam said, "Can you go to Ron Baltimore's music store in Manhattan and pick up a box of saxophone reeds?"

"Sure."

"Bring them back next week."

When I got home Sunday afternoon, my wife was cooking her famous marinara sauce and it smelled great as we sat down to dinner. The meal was delicious and I settled down on the couch afterwards for a nap. But the nap was interrupted by a phone call. Jacqueline came in holding the phone out to me, "It's Sam and he needs to talk to you."

"Sam, what's up?" I said with some concern.

"Bobby, you have to come right back to Atlantic City!"

"Sam, I just got finished eating a big Sunday dinner meal with meatballs, pasta, sausage, and gravy. I'm sacked out on the couch right now."

"Listen, while they were shooting the video on Saturday night, the main director Ezra and the production managers reviewed the video. The band was great. The video was fine, but there was one big problem. The director in the truck outside the hotel had mixed up the solos of each part that the band was playing. There were eight video cameras set up in various places around the area where they were shooting. Each one of the eight cameras had been trained on a different instrument in the band. What was supposed to happen was that as each musician did his solo, the camera in that position was supposed to focus on that musician."

Sam took a breath and I needed one, too.

"But what actually happened was that when the sax player took his solo, the director in the truck clicked on the trumpet player's camera, and when the trumpet player took his solo, the director in the truck clicked on the piano player. The whole video is off sequence. None of the solos match the actual musicians. The sound is askew."

"Don't worry. I'm wide awake now. I'll go back to Atlantic City with Jacqueline and I'll fix everything."

What I realized, unknown to the main director, was that I knew all the songs and every solo of the whole show. I knew Sam's arrangements backwards and forwards. Sam knew it too and he explained to the director that they needed me in the truck to get the whole thing right. After all, this video cost a lot of money.

I was truly Sam's lifeline. As soon as we got there, I went right to the production truck to meet with the director. Right off the bat he said, "I know you don't have any experience with the camera board, but with my help I think we can do this."

Then he put headphones on me and sat me in his chair and we started to contact each cameraman in the show area, cameras one through eight. Sam and the band were ready to rehearse the opening song "When You're Smiling." My job was to watch via the cameras in the truck and rematch the solos with the video. The director in the truck contacted his floor person and said, "Let's make this a go."

As the band started playing, camera number one had a full-screen angle on the band. When the solos began, I started to click on the right camera for the right sequence to match each of solos as they were played. The rehearsal went perfectly and when they played back the tape everything was fine, with every camera matched to the right solo.

The director looked at me with astonishment and shook his head in amazement. "I can't believe that you got the songs and solos to the exact note."

"After hearing those tunes for many years," I told him, "I know them by heart."

"Bobby," he said to me, "we couldn't have completed this video without you!"

How about that?

Sam gave me a hug and said, "See you next week."

With that, I said, "Good night all," and Jacqueline and me started the drive back to the city. It was late when we left Resorts International and about an hour or so into the ride on the Garden State Parkway I started to fall asleep. Jacqueline had to give me a shove to wake me up. I knew if I kept on driving we were going to get hurt or killed in a bad accident, so I pulled over and asked Jacqueline to take the wheel. I fell asleep again, but she was in no better shape than I was. She started to see mountains and a red brick wall in front of her when there weren't any there. She began to sway all over the road. She pulled over, woke me up and said, "I can't drive any further. You have to drive."

Reluctantly, I took the wheel and somehow, we made it home. If I learned one lesson from the experience, it was that I'll never do that again--drive down to Atlantic City and back the same night, especially not after Sunday dinner.

That same year Sam informed me that they were going to do a show from Resorts International called Atlantic City Live, hosted by Bob Eubank. Sam Butera and the Wildest were on the bill for that evening, with

Tony Martin. There was a rehearsal before filming of the live show. Right after that the stagehands set up for the real thing. They positioned the microphones and they set up the lights above the stage.

As I was watching, I noticed where the lights had been placed. They were bright and very hot and I saw sprinkler heads in the ceiling right near them. I knew that if those sprinklers were heated to 125°, they would go off, so I found a stagehand and told him, "Listen fella, I think those lights for the show are too close to the sprinkler heads above the stage."

"Everything will be fine," he said.

"Okay, if you feel that way."

The band was all set to play, and the director gave the signal that they were ready to shoot live. Sam went into his signature song "When You're Smiling," and the crowd was clapping and jumping all over. Sam was giving it his all, completely focused on the audience, so he didn't realize that the sprinkler head above the stage suddenly went off behind him in the middle of the song. He kept playing. He had no idea what was happening. He was still playing when Arnie Tite, the pianist, got up and ran away from the piano. Chuck Stevens left his drums and the rest of the musicians left the stage. The only one left standing there was Sam, who suddenly realized something was wrong, turned around, and saw the stage getting flooded.

That show was never televised, but I do have a copy of the video showing water pouring down on all the instruments. I didn't want to add insult to injury after that, so I never mentioned to Sam that I had warned the stagehand what could happen.

That was the beginning of the end of the *Atlantic City Live* television show. I guess the production of that show wasn't cost effective, to say the least and we were soon informed that the show had been canceled by the production company.

By 1983 I'd seen and experienced enough of the behind-the-scenes production works that I felt that I could produce my own show. I decided the show would be at a college in my area in a venue called the Golden Center. I wanted to do a Columbus Day party, with Sam Butera, Jerry Vale, and Pat Cooper on the bill. I figured this would be a sell-out show with the people from my hometown, so I spoke to Sam to get his buy-in. He said, "Bobby, remember, if the tickets don't sell or you can't make the nut, you're going to have to start writing checks from your personal checking account."

"I'm fine with that, Sam, but I think this bill will work on its own."

I was a little afraid of producing the show for the first time by myself, so I asked Chuck Stevens to be my co-producer. I thought of getting in touch with Pat Cooper, who had worked with Sam numerous times and would be great on the bill. The problem was that I couldn't raise the money to pay for three acts.

"Chuck," I asked, "What do we do now?"

"We have two choices we do the show with Sam and Jerry Vale, or we do the show with Sam and Pat Cooper. You make the decision."

"Before I decide, I'm going to the college. I want to talk to the people there to find out how to go about selling tickets."

Problem after problem arose. We had to pay for the venue, for the stagehands, for the performers, and for the personnel; and we had to rent the piano. Then, what really hit hard was that Ticketmaster wanted thirty percent of ticket sales. So with all of this information, Chuck and me sat down to figure out what the show would cost us. With all of the expenses, we came up with a profit of ten thousand dollars. But that would only be if the entire venue was sold out with a ticket price of $40 to $50 per ticket. At that time that was a lot of money for a single-show ticket.

That was the beginning and the end of my producing shows. I became very conscious how often people go to shows and never really think about what it takes to produce them. As a producer, you can make a good night's pay, but you can also take a bath; and when you have to start writing checks to cover the payroll for these acts, you better have enough dough to cover the bills that night or you'll be spending a lot of days in court being sued. Even so, it would've been a great experience to produce my own show. That became a dream that lingered in my mind for many years. I had both worked and been to many big venues where the producers took on big acts, pinning all their hopes on ticket sales. If they had good ticket sales, they realized a profit at the end the night. But before that could happen, they often had to invest a lot of dough up front for advertising. Buying time on the radio and TV, and space in newspapers, was very costly and they needed a sold-out show.

In my role as a road manager at some venues I interacted with the producer of the show to determine the schedule of the acts. All the assistants and assistants to the assistants had their hands full making sure that everything ran smoothly for that night's show. Some were nervous wrecks. At some venues, there were many empty seats in the audience. Even if producers did have enough capital to pay the acts they still had to write checks for all the other expenses, often for insufficient profit. So as much as I loved the idea of producing my own show, I wasn't able to do so because the financial risk was too great.

CHAPTER 19

One day at the Westchester Premier Frank Sinatra was rehearsing. Sam Butera and The Wildest were opening for him. When Sam and I came into the theater, Frank called Sam up on the stage to have a few words with him. I stayed back, but Sam turned to me, "Come with me and I'll introduce you to Sinatra."

I was a little nervous. "Are you sure about that?"

"Sure, I'm sure."

We got to the stage and Sam said, "Mr. S. this is Bobby Lauri, my road manager."

Sinatra was dressed in navy gabardine slacks and a light blue sport shirt. He smiled his famous smile as he graciously shook my hand.

I was speechless. I don't remember what I said at that time. This man had so much electricity that he could have lit up the entire Las Vegas Strip. With that, he told Sam to have a seat in the theater, so Sam and I sat down in the third or fourth row. As we took our seats, we found ourselves sitting with Pat Henry and Jilly Rizzo. Pat was a well-known comedian and television actor, who often opened Sinatra's show. Jilly Rizzo was a New York restauranteur and Sinatra's closest confidante.

Mr. S. started singing to the four of us, and I was in shock. What would my friends think? I myself was actually thinking of Dean Martin's lyrics "How Lucky Can One Guy Be?"–to be watching Frank Sinatra rehearse his songs for that night's show twelve feet in front of me.

That was the first time I met Frank Sinatra. Sam opened multiple shows for him, and one night Frank called Sam to his dressing room to go over the song that Sam would do when Sam took his solo during Frank's show. When Sam and I knocked on Sinatra's door, he said to come in and as we walked into the dressing room, he told us to make ourselves a drink. As I made a drink, I glanced over at a table in the room filled with octopus—"*pupa*"–salad. It looked delicious. Sinatra looked at me and said, "Bobby, you like that?"

"I love octopus."

"Get a plate and enjoy yourself," he said with a warm smile.

That was the best octopus salad I ever had.

He started talking to Sam and it seemed like he was angry about something. He mentioned to Sam that he was having a problem with his schedule.

Sam said, "Give it to Bobby; he'll handle the problem for you."

I gave Sam a quizzical look to let him know that I was not comfortable with the responsibility. Sinatra handed me his itinerary and said, "Do you want another job while we're in town?"

I smiled. "I already have enough problems with *his* itinerary," jerking my thumb toward Sam, "but thanks, Mr. S., for asking."

With that, we left the dressing room and I said to Sam, "Thanks for putting me on the spot."

"Just think, you could be working for Mr. S."

I laughed. After the show that night Sam told me that there was going to be a dinner party on closing night in the Westchester Premier Theater restaurant. "Frank wants certain people to attend. You're invited to the dinner and you'll sit with me."

I was excited to share this news with my brother-in-law Sally. I invited him to come with me, telling him that if I got up enough nerve, I would introduce him to Mr. S. that night.

Sally came with me to the restaurant. Before dinner Sinatra always came down from his dressing room and had a drink at the bar. I told Sally, "When I walk over to Mr. S. to say hello, stay next to me and I'll introduce you."

Sally loved Frank Sinatra and he wanted to give him the gold cigarette lighter that had been given to him by his cousin Chubby. So Sally and me were in the lounge waiting for Sam; and I noticed Sinatra at the bar having a drink.

I went up to Mr. S. who said, "Hi, Bobby."

I said, "Hi, Mr. S.," and as I turned around to introduce Sally he was nowhere to be found. To cover the awkward moment, I just said, "I'm looking for Sam."

DAY	DATE	CITY	PERFORMANCE	HOTEL
		1976		7/19/76
		SINATRA ENGAGEMENTS CALENDAR		
Fri.	8/20	Palm Springs to Vancouver	Rehearsals	Bayshore Inn
Sat.	8/21	Vancouver, Canada	EXHIBITION PARK	
		After performance fly to New York		Waldorf Astoria
Sun.	8/22	OFF		Waldorf Astoria
Mon.	8/23	New York - 2:00 to 6:00 P.M.		
		Rehearsals NBC Hall #8H		Waldorf Astoria
Tues.	8/24	Saratoga, New York	PERFORMING ARTS CENTER	Waldorf Astoria
		Performance 8:15 P.M.		
Wed.	8/25	Holmdel, New Jersey	GARDEN STATE ARTS CENTER	Waldorf Astoria
Th.	8/26	Holmdel, New Jersey	GARDEN STATE ARTS CENTER	Waldorf Astoria
Fri.	8/27	Clarkston, Mich.	PINE KNOB MUSIC THEATRE	Sheraton-Pontiac
Sat.	8/28	Clarkston, Mich.	PINE KNOB MUSIC THEATRE	Sheraton-Pontiac
Sun.	8/29	Cincinnati, Ohio	RIVERFRONT COLISEUM	
		Performance 8:00 P.M.		
		After performance fly to Palm Springs		
Mon.	8/30	OFF - Palm Springs		
Tues.	8/31	OFF - Palm Springs	(Musicians to Las Vegas for rehearsals)	
Wed.	9/1	Palm Springs to Las Vegas	(Rehearsals)	Caesars Palace
Th.	9/2	Las Vegas	CAESARS PALACE	Caesars Palace
Fri.	9/3	Las Vegas	CAESARS PALACE	Caesars Palace
Sat.	9/4	Las Vegas	CAESARS PALACE	Caesars Palace
Sun.	9/5	Las Vegas	CAESARS PALACE	Caesars Palace
Mon.	9/6	Las Vegas	CAESARS PALACE	Caesars Palace

FRANK'S SCHEDULE

I felt like a fool. I'd planned all this for Sally, whom I loved dearly, and it would have been a wonderful memory for him if he hadn't panicked on me.

When I finally saw Sally just before the show, I said, "Where in hell were you? You left me standing there like a fool. I was very embarrassed."

"Bobby, I couldn't do it. When I saw Sinatra that close to you, I froze like a deer in headlights. I just turned and ran away."

The following night after the show Sinatra had a recording date at Columbia Studios, which was in a church on 33rd Street. Sam asked me to come to the recording session. I was overjoyed to join him.

We entered the studio at about midnight, and Frank was rehearsing the song he was going to record. It was a John Denver song, "Sometimes I Feel like a Sad Song." There had to be at least thirty musicians there, all on string instruments, violins, cellos, and a bass, no brass at all. They had Claus Ogerman, a German conductor who had worked with Billie Holiday.

Sam and me sat in the recording booth with Jilly Rizzo and Barbara Sinatra. I couldn't believe my eyes, me, Bobby Lauri, sitting in that sound booth. TALK ABOUT ME BEING IN THE CIRCLE! I still can't get over the trust that Barbara, Jilly, and Sam had in me to bring me into that recording session. Can you imagine what it felt like to be sitting next to those people? My head was in a cloud; that's what it felt like to me. I did, however, have one clear thought at the moment: *You have to have great pipes, as only Frank Sinatra had, to go into a recording studio and sing as beautifully as he did at one o'clock in the morning after having done two one-hour-and-a-half shows.*

The recording session was winding down and we were getting ready to leave the studio. Sam left first and I followed him out the swinging door. "I'm beat, Sam. I'm going home."

Frank Sinatra was behind me, and as I held the door open for him he must have overheard me say that I was going home. "Hey kid, where're you going? The night is young– we're going to Rocky Lee's Bar. Bobby, you're from this town; show Sam how to get there."

"Okay, Mr. S."

I wasn't going to tell him I was exhausted. I'd have rather died. So Sam and me waited at the front door of Rocky Lee's Bar for Mr. S., Barbara, Jilly Rizzo, Pat Henry, and the five musicians who always accompanied Mr. S.: drummer Irv Cutler, upright bass player Gene Cherico, his conductor and piano player Bill Miller, guitarist Al Viola, and the first trumpet player in the band Charlie Turner.

When Mr. S. and his group pulled up in front of Rocky Lee's, Sam and me went in. I noticed that the manager was approaching the patrons inside to ask them if they would be kind enough to leave right away. It was about 2 a.m. and people were having a late supper. They didn't know what was going on. The manager told them that he was giving a late party for his close friends. His customers were very obliging to him and left their tables. As the place emptied out, it filled up with Sinatra's people.

That night at Rocky Lee's the drinks flowed up and down the bar. Pat Henry sat at the middle of bar with guitar player Al Viola, the guy who played the mandolin on the soundtrack for *The Godfather*. A few other close friends of Mr. S. were sitting there. Mr. S. was standing at the bar.

I was walking when I came near Sinatra unexpectedly. He stopped me and greeted me warmly, so I started to think of something to say. But he first told the bartender, "Give this kid a drink."

The bartender poured me a giant glass of Jack Daniels. I started to sip the drink, hoping it would ease the conversation I was about to have with one of my greatest idols.

What am I going to talk to Frank Sinatra about? I wondered, as the wheels in my head spun. I did ask him, "Why do you only do one or two takes in the recording studio before you ask the band to wrap it up?"

He put his hand on my shoulder. "Some recording artists take a lot of time to get the track right and that drives up the cost of the session. My session costs me $20,000 while some artists wind up paying $80,000."

"That's very interesting."

Pat Henry was sitting in front of us and he turned around to ask Mr. S., "What were you both discussing?"

Mr. S. just looked at him and said, "Enjoy your drink."

I was still sipping my Jack Daniels, and since it was 3 a.m., I said, "I need to go home."

Mr. S. looked at me with his piercing blue eyes, "Why do you have to leave?"

"I'm beat. I don't know where you get the stamina to do a late show and then jump right into a recording session at 1 a.m., and then party."

"Listen, Bobby, I stay at the Waldorf Towers when I'm in town. You get a room there. A friend of mine has a bakery in Hoboken. I'll call him and ask him to send over some nice hot bread in the morning. We can have bread and butter and a cup of coffee."

I smiled. Sinatra could have the best breakfast the Waldorf had to offer and here he's inviting me to have hot Italian bread and butter with coffee. This is what Italian culture is all about. I loved that about him. I later read an article in the paper that said that Sinatra used to call his baker friend Dave in Hoboken, New Jersey, and ask him to ship fifty loaves of Italian bread to Palm Springs, California. There are certain things in life for which there are no substitutes, like having a hot cup of coffee with Italian bread and butter.

I didn't take up Mr. S.'s offer that night to stay at the Waldorf. Before I was about to leave Rocky Lee's, Sam came over to check on me and asked, "How are you doing?"

Sinatra answered for me. "Everything's fine and dandy. We had been talking about the costs of sessions."

Sam left. He figured Frank was enjoying talking to me. Then, Frank's wife Barbara called to him, leaning over the railing of the boutique shop upstairs from the bar. "I want to leave, Frank."

Looking at me, he answered her, "The night is still young. I want to hang out a little longer."

I started to laugh, and he laughed with me. Then, he looked at me and said, "I just can't finish a show and go to sleep because I have to unwind with a drink."

With that, I said, "Goodnight," and I went home.

When Frank was in town, he always spent a night hanging out at Jilly's Saloon in the City. After a show at Westchester Premier Theater one night he told Sam and Sam's friends to meet him at Jilly's for a drink.

I called Jacqueline on the phone. "We're going to Jilly's after the show to hang out. I'd like you to be there. Would you like to join us?"

"Hon, I'm afraid to drive into the City at night. What about asking our friends, Tara and Artie to come? They live near us in Flushing."

"Swell idea."

When Jacqueline asked them, and they heard they would be hanging out with Frank Sinatra and his friends, they were thrilled. They didn't hesitate for a moment to get dressed up. They all piled into Artie's care and he drove them to Jilly's.

The three of them arrived before we did. Joey Rizzo, Jilly's son, was at the door that night and the bar was packed. Someone working in the place stopped Jacqueline and our friends and wanted to know why they were heading to the back area where there was a private party.

Jacqueline said, "We've been invited by Frank Sinatra."

The man apologized and cleared the way for them.

A half-hour later Sam and me arrived, along with Sinatra, Jilly, and Barbara, and we made our way toward the back, where Mr. S. always sat in the last booth on the left side. I greeted Jacqueline and our friends warmly, as you can imagine. They were sitting about ten feet from Frank's table. Sam and I could've sat with him, but we showed respect to my wife and friends and sat with them.

Now, who came walking in but William B. Williams? He was the disc jockey on the WNEW radio show that played all the American standard songs, and he always featured Frank Sinatra records on his show. He was the first guy to call Mr. S. the "Chairman of the Board," a name which stuck. At his table were Frank's conductor Bill Miller and a few friends I did not recognize. We partied all night long.

At one point Frank had to go to the bathroom. Jilly's had a private bathroom upstairs, concealed behind a curtain, for celebrities of his caliber.

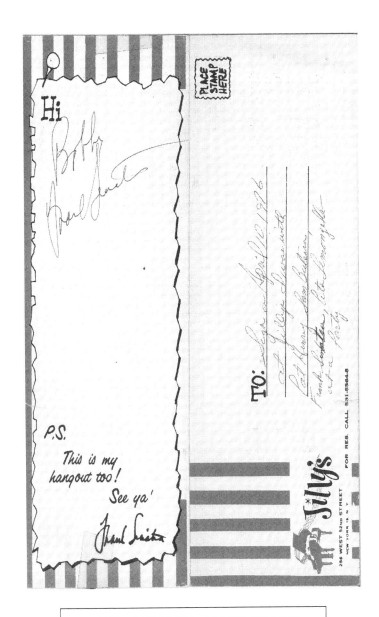

PRIZED SINATRA AUTOGRAPH

Although when I was working with Louie Prima and Sam Butera I met many celebrities, but I never asked any of them for an autograph. It was not the thing to do when you were around these people because you were part of their group and not an autograph-seeker. But that night at Jilly's I broke my own rule.

"Wouldn't it be nice if I could get an autograph from Frank Sinatra on a Jilly's menu?" I asked Jacqueline. "That would be something to have and to keep."

So, when Frank made his move to go upstairs to the bathroom, I was ready with Jilly's menu. I wasn't going act like a stalker, lurking behind the curtain and waiting for him to come out of the bathroom. I had more class than that. I waited a few minutes and then I started to work my way toward the curtain at the back of the room. Just then Frank came down the stairs. I walked over as casually as I could. I said, "Would you mind signing an autograph from me on the menu?"

He made a face and it looked to me like he was annoyed, but he gave me his autograph. Stars like him don't always give out their autographs willingly. I had known that from when I met Joe DiMaggio. Anyway, Mr. S. signed the menu for me.

I returned to my table, where Jacqueline and our friends were sitting sipping drinks. I could tell they were excited about the autographed menu when they all looked at it. Thank God, Sam hadn't witnessed what I'd done, because he would have been angry with me.

Finally, the night ended and we all parted ways. Before we left, I introduced Jacqueline to Barbara Sinatra who was gracious. "It's nice to meet you," she said to Jacqueline with a warm smile.

Sam Butera and the Wildest had been back on tour for a while and were doing very well. Sam called one morning, "The band and I are performing in Atlantic City at Resorts International. Can you come?"

"You can bet I'll be there."

Sam split his year into two halves roughly, twenty-four weeks in Atlantic City and twenty-four weeks in his hometown of Las Vegas, with a month for travel and vacation. Atlantic City started to be real fun for me.

One week when we worked Sam's show in the Rendezvous Lounge at Resorts International, we heard through the grapevine that Sinatra was coming in for a week to work the showroom. That was where I really got to know him. Sam appeared onstage with Frank to perform his song

"Stargazer," which was getting a lot of air play. Frank featured Sam's saxophone solo in that song.

I went backstage and watched Sinatra's whole show from stage right, grinning from ear to ear. Then Sam went off stage and got ready to do his own show.

It happened that one night Gary, the security guard, told me, "Bobby, Barbara Sinatra would like to talk to you."

"What about?"

"I don't know, she's playing blackjack at one of the tables."

I moved around the casino floor and spotted Barbara at a game.

"Barbara," I said, "The security guard told me you were looking for me. What can I do for you?"

"Can you rearrange the show schedule?

"Why?"

"My husband would like to hang out and he wants to take in Sam's show."

"That's easy to do. I'll adjust the schedule".

Now, here's where the fun began. Sam was just about to go on to do his show, which was supposed to be his third and last show of the night.

I went over to him. "Sam, you're going to have to do another show tonight."

"What are you talking about?"

"Barbara Sinatra just asked me if I could make an adjustment to the schedule. The Apple Band will have to start your third show an hour early. Mr. S. will come on your show after he finishes his. After The Apple Band finishes its earlier-than-usual third performance, you'll go on, for a special half-hour add-on and we'll take it from there."

"Okay. I get you."

When the time came, Frank did a surprise walk-on to Sam's late show in the lounge. He came through the casino with a drink in his hand and the crowd went wild. He emptied out the casino. Another soul couldn't fit in the lounge area. Everyone was in shock, and then Frank started to sing "New York, New York."

Afterwards, Sam and I hung out all night until "the wee hours of the morning," the title, in fact, of one of Sinatra's own songs. I finally went to bed about 6:00 a.m.

CHAPTER 20

When Sam played Atlantic City, we stayed at the Seaside Hotel across the street from Resorts International. After the long night, I was just about to go to sleep when I got a phone call from Sam.

"Meet me in the lobby of Resorts International in fifteen minutes."

"What for?"

"Mr. S. wants to see both of us in his room."

"Why?"

"You'll see."

Every time I had met Frank Sinatra before, I was in Sam's company. In orchestra matters he pretty much only talked with Sam. I guessed that Sam maybe needed moral support. We knocked on Frank's door.

He opened it. "Make yourselves drinks, fellas."

Mind you, I had been up all night and had enough Stingers in me to last the whole day. So, we made two Jack Daniels. That's what Mr. S. always drank. Without realizing it I left the cap off the bottle. Boy, did I get a look from Sinatra to remember. He walked calmly over and put the cap back on the bottle.

I understood where he was coming from. Italians have certain quirks, with which I was well familiar. When we had dinner at Aunt Antoinette and Uncle Tom's home, my aunt laid a knife on the table for cutting the meat. Whoever cut the meat had better clean off that knife or they were in trouble. Uncle Tom never tolerated a dirty knife on the table. I also had a brother-in-law, Charles "Dewey" (Albasi). I loved that guy. We lost him at a very young age. Dewey's thing was that if you wanted some bread, you had to cut it with a knife, not tear off pieces with your hands. God forbid you did so, he went off the wall. My family originally came from southern Italy, where bread was always torn with the hands. Knives were used in northern Italy where my brother-in-law came from. I guess they were more high-class up there.

Anyway, Sinatra told Sam why he had called him into his dressing room that morning. I listened as he said, "I'm giving you the first press of my *Trilogy* album. I want you to have the very first copy."

Sam was ecstatic, and I was equally thrilled. I could finally get some sleep without having to handle an emergency.

MY OFFICIAL ID

A few days later my son Michael and his friend came for a visit. They stayed at the Seaside Hotel with us. The boys were having a blast in the pool with some band members. The piano player was Arnie Tite, who played with Dean Martin and had also been the music director for the great comedienne Totie Fields. When she passed away at the young age of forty-eight, Arnie went to work with Sam and stayed with him until Sam retired.

Another band member, Chuck Stevens, was the brother of Connie Stevens. I became very close with Chuck. I came to consider him, in fact, my best friend. Chuck and I often shared a room together when we were on the road.

Mr. S. was performing that night at Resorts International. Before the show started, I brought Michael backstage so he would have a bird's eye view of Frank. Michael was standing so close backstage during the show that he told me later he had the feeling Mr. S. was looking straight at him.

ME AND CHUCK STEVENS

When Mr. S. sang "New York, New York," my son's eyes lit up with joy. Who wouldn't give his right arm to be as close to Frank Sinatra singing his most iconic song?

One of Frank's closest friends was Joe Raposo, who played first violin. Joe wrote many of *Sesame Street*'s well-known songs, including the "Sesame Street Theme and the theme songs for '70s TV sitcoms *Three's Company* and *The Ropers*. I got to know him very well, along with upright bass player Gene Cherico; drummer Irv Cutler, who had also been a recording-session musician for Bing Crosby, Louie Armstrong, and Ella Fitzgerald; guitarist Tony Mottola, who, after being with Sinatra for years, later joined , Tonight Show Band; and first trumpet Charles Turner.

Sinatra always carried these five musicians with him in his concerts. Between shows Joe often said to me, "Bobby, try to get a couple of guys together for a poker game." I gathered up six or seven people from the band and we played poker between shows backstage in the dressing room. It was fun to be with these guys. Besides being immensely talented musicians, they knew how to have a good time.

After a few years Frank got used to seeing me around backstage with Sam. Sometimes Sam and me were the only ones backstage near him and his security guard. I watched his show every night standing in the same place. He never spoke to me but he knew I was there. Comedian Charlie Callas often opened the show, and Frank heckled him in jest from stage right,

"Come on, Charlie; hurry the hell off!"

Charlie heard him and muttered something to the audience about the treatment he was getting from Frank. He turned to Frank and made light of Frank's heckling, and then it was Frank's turn to take the stage and dazzle the audience with his famous voice.

I worked the Atlantic City shows on weekends, and I went home on Monday mornings. I worked at my job in the City Tuesdays through Thursday mornings and left again on Thursday afternoon for Atlantic City. When Jacqueline was able to, she came back with me for the weekend. We had become close friends with Chuck Stevens and his wife Kim and the four of us often spent time together in Atlantic City.

One day Jacqueline and Kim were poolside at our hotel across the street from Resorts International when they saw a flatbed trailer pull up to Resorts International carrying a huge birthday cake. They later found out that Mr. S. had ordered the cake as a surprise for Pat Henry's birthday party. Pat Henry was the comedian, and opening act for Sinatra. But there was more to the surprise.

Mr. S. called me over after the show that night. "Bobby, I'm giving a birthday party for Pat Henry tomorrow night, and I want you to tell Sam that I want him to emerge out of this giant cake I got and sing 'Happy Birthday' to Pat."

When I told this to Sam, he raised his voice and squealed, "I ain't jumpin' outta no cake!"

"You'll have to tell Sinatra that."

That night we all went backstage and put Sam and his saxophone in the cake. Sinatra was there too, watching as we wheeled the cake into the restaurant where the surprise party was to be held. When the guests started singing "Happy Birthday" to Pat Henry, out popped Sam, wailing the song on his tenor sax.

T

JACQUELINE AND KIM

The following weekend there was another party in one of Resorts International main ballrooms to celebrate the retirement of the hotel's president, James Crosby. Sam was one of the scheduled entertainers for the party, along with many other notable celebrities. When Sam and the band entered the ballroom, they were in full band dress in blue jackets with white pants. Sam wore a red jacket and white pants. Sinatra and me were standing next to each other, and when Mr. S. noticed that Sam wasn't wearing a tuxedo, he turned to me and said, "Bobby, couldn't you get Sam to dress up in a tux?"

"Mr. S., I offered to give him my tux."

That was true. I had offered Sam my tuxedo because he'd told me that he hadn't brought his from Las Vegas. Frank tapped me gently on the cheek, indicating that he understood what I was trying to tell him. After Sam performed, Frank told him, "There's not too many of us left in show business who wear tuxes anymore, but you should've somehow gotten one."

When the renovation of Carnegie Hall in New York was completed in 1986, Sinatra and a long list of other talented musicians performed for the re-opening. World-renowned violinist Isaac Stern was the Carnegie president at the time and was also one of the performers at that concert.

Before the show Isaac Stern was rehearsing onstage while Frank Sinatra, some of his friends, and me watched in the audience. Someone mentioned that it was Isaac Stern's birthday and Mr. S. said to me, "Bobby, go to my dressing room and bring down a shoebox that's on the chest of drawers."

I returned with the shoebox. "Here it is."

"Give this to Isaac," Mr. S said.

Mr. Stern was still onstage, and as I approached him from the audience, he had to lean down to me. I offered up the shoebox, saying, "This is a Happy Birthday gift from Mr. Sinatra."

I watched as he opened the shoebox. "Oh how wonderful," he said. "It's a miniature violin and bow." He started laughing, waved his hand to Frank, and called out, "Thank you, Mr. S!"

***

When Jacqueline was with me in Atlantic City, she loved to play the slots. I loved walking the boardwalk. I strolled past the 600 room Ritz-Carlton, where Enoch L. "Nucky" Johnson had lived and had his office. "Nucky" had been very popular in Atlantic City politics from the early 1900s until the 1940s. Every time I walked past the redbrick structure of the Ritz-Carlton, I stopped and read some of what was written on the plaque on the front wall of the hotel. "Presidential guests included Calvin Coolidge, Warren G. Harding, and Herbert Hoover. Other famous guests included Al Capone, Enoch "Nucky" Johnson, Lucky Luciano, Lawrence Tibbet, Sophie Tucker, and NY Mayor Jimmy Walker."

I walked inside the ornate lobby of the hotel with its grand staircase and marble floors every chance I got, looking at pictures of "Nucky" and his political friends and of Atlantic City and the celebrations there in the 1920s and 1930s.

My walk every morning on the Atlantic City boardwalk was from the Tropicana to the Revel Hotel. One week Justin Timberlake was appearing at the Revel, and he was on the boardwalk doing a photo shoot. I walked past but didn't want to disrupt his work, so I walked around the hotel for a little while. As I was leaving, I bumped into him and his wife Jessica Biel. Since we were now face to face, I said, "Hello Mr. Timberlake, I didn't want to disturb you while you were doing your shoot on the boardwalk. I used to be a road manager for Louie Prima and Sam Butera, and through Sam Butera I had the pleasure of meeting Frank Sinatra."

With that, I started to walk away from them, but Jessica Biel called me back. I may have been mistaken, but she seemed more interested in talking about Frank Sinatra than in chatting with me. That would have been understandable, but I said just the same, "See you around," and I went on my way.

The following week on our way home from Atlantic City Jacqueline and me stopped in upper New Jersey to have dinner with my son and his family. I asked my granddaughter Sophia if she'd ever heard of a guy named Justin Timberlake.

"Grandpa," she screamed, "Where did you see him?"

"I ran into him and his wife Jessica Biel in front of the Revel in Atlantic City."

"Grandpa, did you get his autograph for me?"

"I didn't think you'd heard of him. The next time I see him I promise I'll try to get you an autograph."

Years later, when I would watch the TV series *Empire Boardwalk* every week, I got nostalgic for the place I'd visited on so many occasions. The Ritz-Carlton was converted into luxury condominiums in 1982, but it has still kept the look of Atlantic City in its heyday.

CHAPTER 21

In the first chapter I wrote about the time I gave Frank Sinatra a set of my trains. Now I'll finish that story.

When I got home, I spoke to my wife and kids. "I told Frank Sinatra about the trains just before his show. He said he'd like them."

They looked at me as if I had two heads.

"Dad," Michael said. "That's hard to believe."

The next day Sinatra's secretary Dorothy called me at home. "Mr. Sinatra is quite interested in the trains. He told me to give you a call about them."

"I'll be sure to bring them this week."

After the call my kids believed me.

Before I left on Thursday, Dorothy called again and reminded me to please bring the trains, as Mr. S. was driving her crazy and wouldn't stop asking her about them.

"I'll bring the trains to him but I don't want to barge in on him while he's rehearsing."

When I spoke to Sam about it, I told him I hoped he wasn't angry at me for asking Frank about the trains without asking him first.

What he said next made me jump with joy, "Sinatra knows you, and if he didn't think he could trust you to be in his presence, he would have said something."

"Dorothy called my house and told me to bring the trains at night to Mr. S.'s dressing room."

"Sounds like a good plan," Sam said.

Jacqueline came with me to Atlantic City that weekend, and before I left my hotel room to deliver the trains, I asked her, "Please come with me. I need support."

"This is your thing and I'm too nervous to be there with you. You'll be all right by yourself."

Before I went, I had a shot of bourbon at the Seaside Hotel bar. As I walked across the street to Resorts International, a couple of casino dealers were having a smoke. One said to me, "Hey, you're the guy who's going to give a train set to Frank Sinatra."

"How do you know?"

The dealer said, "The whole casino staff heard about Sam Butera's road manager giving Frank trains." He held open the door to the casino for me like I was President of the United States. I walked through the casino and people and dealers looked at me. I felt kinda foolish carrying this box in both hands on my way to the elevator to Mr. S.'s dressing room.

A cocktail waitress with a very short skirt grabbed my arm and said, "Bobby, can we come with you?"

"No, I'm so nervous I don't need more people around me."

When I reached the floor where Frank's dressing room was, I saw a security guard in a casino uniform with a shiny badge. He stopped me. "You're the guy with the trains."

"Yeah! You said it."

"Mr. Sinatra is waiting for you."

I walked over to the door that had a big star and Frank Sinatra's name. I put the box down on the floor in front of me. I knocked on the door. When I heard him say, "Come in," I opened the door and right before my eyes was the man himself. Frank Sinatra greeted me. "Fix yourself a drink."

"Thanks."

I made myself a bourbon and water. Joe Parnell, Frank's musical conductor, was playing a piano in the suite and Frank went over to him.

"Joe Parnell this is Bobby Lauri."

"Hi. Pleased to meet you," I said, and then I opened the box. The first train I pulled out was the engine. I watched Frank's face as I handed it to him. He had a grin on him like a kid in a candy store.

At that moment the door opened and in walked Nancy Sinatra and Frank's body guard, Robert Palomino.

Nancy looked in the box and said, "It's those things."

I looked at Frank and didn't say a word.

Frank said, "Bobby, pay no attention to Nancy. The trains bring back bad memories for her. When she was a kid, there was an incident with Frank Junior involving trains. It had a bad effect on her."

I started to take the other trains out of the box: the box car, the red dumper, the oiler car, the coal car, and the caboose. As I gave each one to Frank, he commented how clean they were. In his eyes they looked brand new, though they were forty years old. The reason they kept so well was that Nancy, my mother-in-law, had wrapped each and every car beautifully in a cloth. I didn't even notice that Frank had a photographer in the room taking pictures.

After a good couple of minutes, he said to the photographer, "That's enough," and the photographer left the room.

The next night I was with Sam and the band in the dressing room when Sinatra's bodyguard Bobby Palomino came in and told me, "The Boss wants to see you in his dressing room."

My knees started to shake. I looked at Sam and saw the worry on his face. Sam said he would see me later and got ready to do his show. As Bobby Palomino and me walked to Mr. S.'s dressing room, all I could think about was what I must've done wrong. What could I have said that he wanted to see me? My mind was racing as we got off the elevator. There was that security guard again.

I asked Frank's bodyguard, "Are you going to come in with me?"

"No, you're on your own. Good luck."

I knocked on the door, and when I heard Frank say, "Come in," I opened the door and asked him, "Is anything the matter?"

"Make yourself a drink, Bobby."

That's a man with class. As he was putting on his bow tie, he said, "Please wrap the trains up the way they had been in the box. When the Atlantic City gig is over, I can put them on my plane back to Palm Springs."

That was what he wanted. I was so relieved! Now I could tell Sam what Frank wanted. I found Sam in the lobby and spoke softly, "Mr. S. just asked me to pack up the trains for him. Everything is cool."

Sam smiled at me and said, "Bobby, you sure know how to meet people and get things done."

At the end of the week, when Mr. S. had flown the trains back to Palm Springs, they were added to the train layout that he kept in a caboose on his estate. I later found out that there was a book published in 1987 called *Great Toy Train Layouts of America* written by Tom McComas and James Tuohy. My friend, Jimmy Venieris, who was also a collector of toy trains, gave me a copy of the book. Sinatra's layout had been designed by Paul Kirby, who owned a popular model train store in San Dimas, California. Kirby replicated a huge, well-known 1940's Lionel showroom layout for Mr. S., including ceiling-high mountains and the Mississippi River to scale.

I saw my trains on page 137 of Tom McComa's and James Tuohy's book. The first car was the engine, which had been the first smoking engine made. The second car was the coal car; the third and fourth cars were oilers; the fifth was the red coal car dumper; the sixth was the box car; and the last car was the caboose, which lit up. I was so happy that I was the one who gave Mr. S. the trains.

The sale of Frank Sinatra's property after his death had the stipulation that the train collection would go with the property and would remain intact. To this day my trains are still on display in the caboose house where he and his friends enjoyed them.

Things were really going my way in life. I loved working with Sam Butera and the Wildest. Like Louie Prima Sam placed a lot of trust in me. In return he commanded my absolute loyalty. He trusted me in any situation: with the people he introduced me to in show business and with all of his business associates. It was a far cry from my being the boy who couldn't do anything right.

CHAPTER 22

As much as I didn't like bothering the celebrities I met, sometimes they actually invited it like the time Frank Sinatra was working the Westchester Premier Theater with Dean Martin. The two had met as co-stars in the 1958 movie *Some Came Running* and as part of the group of celebrity friends known as "the Rat Pack," they'd performed together many times over the years. Their show combined music and comedy, a lot of which revolved around Dean Martin's reputation and stage persona as a heavy drinker.

Jacqueline was with me for one show.

"Hon," she begged. "I really want to take a picture with Dean Martin."

"I'll have to figure out a way to get you backstage before the show. It won't be easy."

Suddenly before I could come up with a plan, Dean Martin's dressing-room door opened. There was a man sitting next to Jacqueline who smiled and introduced himself as Greg Garrison, the producer of *The Dean Martin* Show. That was Dean's weekly TV variety show and in which his famous celebrity "roasts" took place. Mr. Garrison said, "I'll be happy to send you up to take a picture with Dean when he comes out."

Jacqueline grabbed hold of my hand and squeezed it hard. I was so glad for her.

When Dean came out of his dressing room a short while later, I was doing my pre-show work backstage. "Mr. Martin, I'm Bobby Lauri, the road manager for Sam Butera. Will you be so kind to take a picture with my wife?

As far as I could tell, he was stone-cold sober. He gave me a broad smile, "Where is your wife?

"Mr. Garrison said he'll send Jacqueline up."

Dean and my wife are in such a beautiful picture. Jacqueline treasures it.

JACQUELINE AND DEAN

Unbelievably, Dean turned to me. "Would you like to take a picture with me, too?"

"Well, as Sam Butera's road manager I don't usually take pictures with celebrities because I don't want to bother them."

"Come on, take a picture with me!"

So I did.

Then, he got the cue that the props for the show were being brought out. There was a table with the bottles of booze, glasses, and a bucket of ice. As Dean went on stage, he asked Frank Sinatra in a loud, slurred voice if it was Frank who had called for room service. The crowd applauded and laughed their heads off!

On an earlier trip to Las Vegas I went to the Hilton Hotel off the Vegas Strip, where a fellow by the name of Elvis Presley was performing in the main showroom for a cover charge of ten dollars. I was playing craps one night outside of the showroom when out of the blue the comedienne Ruth Buzzy approached me, tucked her arm in my arm, and said, "Hey handsome, stop throwing your money away and come hang out with us!"

As she walked me to the bar, another guy joined up with us and introduced himself as Alan Sues. At that time there was a popular TV show called *Laugh In* and both Ruth and Alan were regulars on that show. We all had a few drinks and I told Ruth, "I'm going back to play some Baccarat."

As I took a seat at the Baccarat table, another popular comedian of that time, Red Foxx, sat down right next to me. We greeted each other before the card game started. Mr. Foxx was betting a nice piece of change on a hand right next to me, while I bet $50 a hand, which was a lot of money in those days, certainly it was for me.

Red Foxx turned to me and said, "Why don't you follow me? When I bet banker, you bet banker; and when I bet player, you bet player."

He must have noticed that I'd been losing. Once I started following his moves, I started winning. After an hour, I'd won $500. Mr. Foxx had won thousands.

"Red," I said, "thank you very much, but I think I'm going to leave with my winnings now."

"You're a smart kid," he told me. We shook hands and I left.

I regretted that night at the Hilton that I didn't get to see the Elvis Presley show. It often has re-runs on public television, and every time I see it, I get angry at myself all over again.

I hadn't played a gig of my own in years when out of the blue Mario, an old friend of mine, called me at home.

"Hi, Bobby, do you want to play Friday night in Ponte's restaurant in the City on Desbrosses Street? I'm playing the violin and I can use you to fill in for my accordion player. We stroll among the diners with our instruments. I thought you might get a kick out of this."

"I don't know. Now I play just for my own enjoyment. I haven't done a gig in a long time."

"Can't you help me out? I really need you. I don't know anyone else besides you who can possibly help me at the last minute. Please give it a try?"

"Okay," I agreed. *What else could I have said?*

On a freezing Friday night in the middle of the winter I met Mario at Ponte's. We did a rundown of what we were going to play. As we were walking through the dining room on the second floor, I passed an attractive lady dining alone.

"Please, will you play a request for me?"

"What song?"

"I like 'Memories' from the movie *The Way We Were*."

The woman gave me a big smile when we played it. After we finished the set, I saw that the woman was at the exit getting ready to leave the restaurant. She had put on a mink hat and a long fur coat, at the bottom of which were six-inch long mink tails around the hem.

I wanted to speak to her again so I went outside. "The words of the song you requested have a lot of meaning."

She nodded. "Please, would you mind staying with me until my cab comes?"

"It'll be my pleasure." *She's someone special, but I can't put my finger on it.*

When her cab arrived she said, "Thank you. Good night."

I went back into the restaurant to join Mario. On my way to the stage, Angelo Ponte, the owner of the place, stopped me. "Do you know who you were talking with outside while she was waiting for her cab?"

"I didn't get the lady's name. She wasn't very talkative."

Angelo's eyes widened. "That was Greta Garbo, the great film actress during the 1920's and 1930's. I remember what she used to say in a low voice in her Swedish accent 'Life would be so wonderful if we only knew what to do with it.'"

Now it all made sense, especially with that mink hat and long beautiful coat with the mink tails. I couldn't believe I met a genuine movie star who asked for my protection, and I gave it, waiting with her until her cab came. I laughed and went back to playing the accordion.

Something about that brief meeting with Greta Garbo stayed with me, and that night I couldn't sleep. All I could think about was how I had begun: a local nobody from Queens with a miserable father who hated me.

Now I had become part of the entertainment industry; I was a constant companion to one of my idols; and I was meeting and even befriending big celebrities and movie stars. I couldn't help but ask myself: *How had everything turned around so completely? How did I get so lucky? Why have I deserved this? It must be a reward that God Himself has planned. He knew how I felt about show business and the entertainment world, and by His grace He has allowed me to be accepted by these people and become part of their lives, especially after being rejected by my own family. This was too big to have happened by my own hand. The Holy Spirit guided my life and brought me what I need. He brought me the happiness of gaining a lifestyle I'd never even dreamed about.*

* * *

I was still working with Sam in Atlantic City some time later when I found out through the grapevine that the former middleweight champion Rocky Graziano was working as a greeter at the Atlantis Hotel next to the convention center. I decided to go say hello. When I approached him at the Atlantis, I said, "I'm Bobby Lauri. You probably don't remember me, but we met years ago when you were managing the boxer Lenny Mangiapane, a good friend of mine."

I had grown up with Lenny in my old neighborhood. He was one of the sons of the family who owned the bakery in Corona, where I'd worked baking bread and delivering it.

"I do remember you," Rocky said. "How is Lenny? What are you doing in Atlantic City?"

"Lenny's good. I'm Sam Butera's road manager. He's appearing at Resorts International."

Rocky looked interested. "Please will you save me some seats for Sam's show up front at the Rendezvous Lounge, so I can bring my wife Norma and my daughter Audrey to see Sam perform?"

"No problem. Come for the eleven o'clock show tonight and my wife Jacqueline will be holding the seats for you and your family."

That night my wife and me sat with the Grazianos during the show. Sam saw us and announced to the audience that Rocky Graziano and his family were there. Everyone went wild with applause. The show ended and as Jacqueline and me were saying our goodnights to the Grazianos, Rocky said, "Bobby, I'm not much of a beach person. Would you mind doing me a big favor tomorrow?"

"What is it?"

"Will you go with my wife and daughter to the beach tomorrow and sit with them to make sure nobody bothers them so they can enjoy themselves."

"With pleasure. We'll meet at your hotel around noon."

The next day I went with Rocky's family to the beach by the Atlantis Hotel and had a great time. Afterwards, Rocky and me made a plan to meet during the week in the city for breakfast. It turned out that he was an Atlantic City weekender like me. It became a regular thing for me to meet Rocky Graziano and his friends in Manhattan each weekday morning from Monday through Thursday at Rocky's favorite coffee shop for breakfast.

A few years later Rocky passed away. My heart sank as I went to his wake in the City. I walked in, and as I said my condolences to Norma, Audrey, and her sister, I observed something unusual for a wake. A recording of Louis Armstrong singing "Sunny Side of the Street," one of

Rocky's favorite songs, was playing on repeat. When I took my seat, Robert Merrill, the opera singer who used to sing the national anthem before Yankees' games at Yankee Stadium, came and sat next to me. He knew me from Sam's shows in Atlantic City.

"Robert," I said, "it was a great idea to play the song that Rocky loved so much."

He said, "Rocky didn't want anyone to cry at his wake."

The song played over and over. I had two feelings, one was sad that he died and the other was glad that I had known him.

CHAPTER 23

Besides being a road manager and meeting famous people I met quite a few on my job. In 1976, I was working for Metro Control Associates, a large temperature control company with most of its contracts in the City and clients who were among the wealthiest in the country. It really gave me a peek into their personalities and I saw how the "other half" live.

I was working at a new construction job in Manhattan in a building that was owned by Jack and Lewis Rudin, two brothers who were among the biggest commercial builders and real estate moguls in the City, and who were well known in New York society circles.

I was a shop steward at that job and I met with the Rudins at various job meetings. Once Mr. Jack Rudin asked, "How's the job coming along?"

"Things are fine as long as there isn't a problem with the work."

Then Mr. Lewis Rudin asked, "Are you happy here?

"I sure am."

We got to be on a first name basis. Every so often Jack Rudin supplied breakfast for all the workers at the meeting. The men enjoyed it, and that certainly helped the meeting go smoothly.

I never knew where I'd be working or who I'd meet when I got there. One day I got a call to go to the Helmsley Lincoln Towers. I walked into the lobby and a man at the front desk asked if he could help me. I told him I was from Metro Control Associates, and he directed me to the office of Harry Helmsley on the eighth floor. When the elevator doors opened and I stepped out, it felt like I was walking into a sauna. There were about ten or twelve women in the eighth-floor office and when I walked in, they all looked at me eagerly and asked if I was the heating man. I told them I was.

"Please do something," they begged, "It's eighty-five degrees in here!"

"Do you know where the thermostat is?" I asked.

"It's in Mr. Helmsley's office."

I knocked on his office door. Mr. Harry Helmsley in a deep voice said, "Enter."

I exchanged introductions with Mr. Helmsley. "Mr. Helmsley, your girls are complaining that it's too hot in the office. They're sweating and they want me to lower the temperature."

Mr. Helmsley pulled up the waist of his pants with both hands as he said, "Do it."

"Okay. Have a nice day!" I said.

Another time I got a call to go to the home of Jack Heinz, one of the owners of the Heinz Corporation – as in Heinz ketchup. As I approached the door of the huge home on Sutton Place and East 57th Street, I saw an elderly man walk down his front steps. I noticed that he was wearing one blue and one black sock. As he walked toward his waiting limousine, I wondered if I should tell him that his socks didn't match.

"Mr. Heinz, I hope you don't mind my telling you that you're wearing two different colored socks."

He put his hand on my shoulder in a friendly way. "Son, at my age things like that don't matter anymore." Then he gave me a huge smile. "Mrs. Heinz is the house. She'll tell you what has to be fixed."

I couldn't believe what a nice guy he was. I figured as I went into the grand home that this would be a pleasant job. Mrs. Heinz's first name was Drew. As I walked into the large, immaculate kitchen, the chef directed me to her bedroom. I knocked on the door and a woman called out in a gravelly voice, "Come in."

Mrs. Heinz was sitting up in bed talking on the phone, "How's the weather today in London? Raining again? Too bad. I'm working on the details of this week's party. Hold on, I have to talk to a worker here."

I thought, *this bedroom looks like a movie set.*

Mrs. Heinz patted her thinning hair. "Check the thermostat on the wall."

I looked but I couldn't find a thermostat anywhere in the room. "Where is the thermostat?"

Mrs. Heinz pointed to a place behind a velvet cloth. *I had never seen a thermostat hidden like that.*

After I calibrated the thermostat I asked Mrs. Heinz, "Would you like me to surface mount it?"

"No," she said abruptly.

"Have a nice day," I replied. That was the day I learned that rich people have their own way of doing things.

I got a call to go to the Mellon residence, a huge fourteen-room townhouse on East 70th Street, owned by banking heir Paul Mellon. The French-style house had been designed with gardens in the front and back. A reflecting pool and gazebo were in the back garden—something you definitely don't see every day in the heart of Manhattan. I knocked on the door and a tall heavy man opened it.

"Are you the control man?" he said in a booming voice.

"Yeah, I am."

"I'll lead you to the room."

I followed him to the HVAC (Heating, Ventilation, and Air Conditioning) room. Then he left me to do my work.

I checked the air flow in each room. When I was finished working I made my way through the house. There was a large formal dining room, a library and study, and rooms just for staff.

In the hallway, I met a man who greeted me. "I'm Paul Mellon, the owner of this home. It's a pleasure to meet you. Has the chef given you lunch?"

"No sir."

"Then tell him I said to give you a hearty lunch."

This was a memorable experience and I did enjoy the house and the lunch.

My boss, Bobby Farina, asked me a few days later to check out a problem at the Trump Building. The doorman directed me to the right floor, and when I got there and knocked on the ornate door, Ivana Trump opened it. She wore a mink coat. I could hardly believe my eyes. I looked at one gorgeous gal with long thick blond hair.

Mrs. Trump spoke with a Czech accent, "It's freezing inside. Can you please fix what's wrong?"

A few minutes later Donald Trump came out and watched what I was doing. He seemed interested in the procedure, but he didn't utter a word.

After I fixed the problem I said to Mr. and Mrs. Trump, "Glad to have been of help. Good-bye."

One morning I was working a job at Manhattan's Central Synagogue which was in a five-story building. I was waiting for the elevator and when it came I stepped in. Just as the door was about to close, I saw a tall man put his hand in to hold back the door. Quickly I hit the open button. It hit me like a bombshell that it was none other than Cary Grant, the handsome charming movie star.

"Thank you," he said in a gracious manner. "I'm looking for the manufacturer who makes handmade shoes and I don't know which floor it's on. Will you please hold the elevator door while I look on each floor for the right place?"

"I will," I said. I would have done anything for Cary Grant.

After two or three floors, he found the floor where they made shoes by hand.

"Thanks for your help," he said as he left the elevator.

I was speechless. I couldn't even say goodbye.

That night when I went home and told Jacqueline that I met Cary Grant, she went wild, jumped up and down, and shouted, "You met Cary Grant? You lucky son of a gun. Why wasn't I there?"

Another time I got a call to go to one of the major city hospitals to check the temperature in a room with an out-of-control thermostat. At the nursing station I said, "I'm here to fix the thermostat."

"Follow me," the nurse said as she brought me to a room. I looked at a man lying in a hospital bed with his hand in a fracture-brace.

When the nurse left the room, I started to work on the thermostat making some small talk with the patient in the bed. "Do you want the temperature raised or lowered?"

He sat up. "Whatever you decide is fine with me."

He looked like a famous person who I couldn't place. I stared at his face. Wonder of wonders! The man in the bed was none other than Marlon Brando!

Later I learned that Mr. Brando had had a run-in with one of the paparazzi photographers. When he punched the guy, not only did he break his finger, but it got infected and he had to go to the hospital.

At home Jacqueline screamed, "First Greta Garbo, then Cary Grant, and now Marlon Brando. Are you sure you're not making this up?"

"I'm just a lucky guy," I laughed.

In 1980 Metro received a contract to redo Gracie Mansion, the residence of New York City's Mayor Ed Koch. It needed a completely new air-conditioning system. The job was assigned to me and my buddy, Bobby Santo. It involved a total renovation of all AC units, and there were workers of various other trades doing the job with us.

When any project of that scale got finished at Gracie Mansion, the mayor usually celebrated with a big party for his entire political circle. Mayor Ed *"How am I doing?"* Koch had greeted us tradesmen every morning. When the job was finished, he did something very unusual. Instead of giving a party for just his political friends, he invited all the workers who rebuilt the mansion and their wives to a private party. Can you imagine what kind of a man he was to do that? He was a gentleman at heart and we all loved him. Not every New York City mayor did things like that.

The party was given in a large ballroom. We had a beautiful catered dinner with a fancy spread and all the top-shelf wines and booze you could drink. Bobby Santo and his wife met Jacqueline and we all felt like celebrities ourselves.

To start off the evening I handed Jacqueline a glass of white wine, and I picked up a small cherry tomato from the buffet and took a bite. The tomato juice from the little tomato flew through the air and hit Jacqueline right on her dazzling white top. She looked at the tomato stain in shock.

"I'm so sorry," I said with a red face. But Bobby and his wife burst out laughing. After that the evening went on just fine. We toured the whole mansion, took pictures with Mayor Koch, had a great time, and now we have happy memories.

The Mayor of the City of New York

Edward I. Koch
and
Mrs. Joan K. Davidson

Chairman of the Gracie Mansion Conservancy

request the pleasure of your company

at a reception

to preview the historic renovation of

Gracie Mansion

Sunday, the fourth of November

5:00 - 7:00 p.m.

ME AND MAYOR KOCH

One balmy spring night Sam played Westbury with Pat Cooper. They put on a great performance and the audience gave them a standing ovation. After Sam's show a sweet, gray-haired woman was brought backstage with her sister.

My son Michael and his wife Fran were with me that night. Michael immediately recognized the woman as Catherine Scorsese, Martin Scorsese's mother. I knew that Martin Scorsese had been born in Queens and had directed one of my favorite films *Taxi Driver*. He was also a producer, a screenwriter, an actor, and a film historian. His mother had become recognizable through her appearances in her son's films *Goodfellas* and *Casino*.

I greeted her with a warm kiss on the cheek. "Mrs. Scorsese, how are you?"

"I'm fine," she said with a smile.

Michael asked me if I thought Mrs. Scorsese might take a picture with him. I politely asked, "Mrs. Scorsese, "I'm with the Sam Butera show. Would you be so kind as to take a picture with my son Michael?"

"Absolutely." She took a picture with Michael, who was bursting with joy.

MY SON, MICHAEL, AND MRS. SCORSESE

Sam and the boys did eight-week stints in Atlantic City. It was 1994 when Sam told me we were going to do a gig with Jerry Vale in Poughkeepsie, New York. I loved when Jerry with his velvet-voice sang "Arriverderci" in Italian.

Before the show Sam, Jerry, me and the whole crew went to an Italian restaurant in town for dinner. Jerry invited Sam and me to sit with him at his table. We all ordered our food: eggplant *parmigiana,* hero sandwiches, meatballs, and pasta.

As we were eating, I leaned over and asked Jerry, "Who's going to be performing first?" He answered, "During rehearsal I discussed this with the show's producer who said Sam will be the opening act."

"Look, Jerry, why don't you go first? Let Sam close the show."

"We'll see at show time," he said.

Back at the hotel before the show I heard that Jerry had been giving some thought to my suggestion. I stopped in to see Sam and told him what I had mentioned to Jerry about his opening the show and letting Sam close.

Sam said to me, "You know, he's the star of this show and he won't relinquish the closing spot to me."

"Sam," I said, "listen to what I think. The only star *you* can open for without a problem is Frank Sinatra. In my opinion, in the case of any other performer you open for, you bring the level of the show to such a high that the second act, which is supposed to be the main attraction, doesn't feel right. It's not that the act isn't good, it's just that it gets overshadowed."

Sam told me to leave it the way it was scheduled. After my sound check with the stagehands, the show started at 8:00 p.m. with Sam Butera and the Wildest. It opened, to a packed house, with Sam's "When You're Smiling." The audience started screaming and clapping their hands and singing along with Sam. I was standing at stage left when all of a sudden Jerry Vale appeared behind me and said to me, "Bobby, where in the hell does he get all that energy from?"

At that point he must've been having second thoughts about what we'd spoken about at dinner regarding the order of the show. But it was too late now. "*Que sera, sera.*"

After Sam and the band finished, Jerry's orchestra started tuning up. The curtain was closed and Jerry was standing next to me backstage. I wished him a good show and with that the announcer said, "Ladies and gentlemen, let's give a warm welcome to the star of the show, Jerry Vale!"

The audience applauded as Jerry came out and started singing his greatest hits, including "Pretend You Don't See Her At All," "*O Sole Mio*", "*Inamorata*", and "*Al di là*". He was in perfect form and his voice was as mellow as you can get with every note in perfect tone. But as good as Jerry was, Sam had left the crowd on a high and Jerry's singing was a bit of a let-down, as I had predicted. All and all the performances were terrific.

After the show we parted. The following year Sam and Jerry were on the same bill again for a show at the Westbury Music Fair. Jerry came to see me backstage and said, "Bobby, tell Sam I'm going first."

Sam, of course, agreed readily and Jerry opened the show. The crowd loved him and his voice was superb as he sang the songs he'd made famous. After Jerry finished, Sam went on and blasted the people out of their seats. Jerry was standing next to me watching him, and said, "This is the way we should have done it in Poughkeepsie."

"Jerry, I said, "we learn from experience."

After the successful Westbury show Jerry invited me out to Palm Springs. He wanted Jacqueline and me to move out there to be near him and his wife Rita.

"I'll look for a condo for you close to mine so we can play cards every day together," he said.

"That sounds great, but the only problem is my wife. If you can get my wife to move out to California, you and me can retire together in Palm Springs."

The move never took place. Years later, Jerry had a stroke and my heart wept for him. I loved that guy. He was extraordinarily friendly to me. He had taken a liking to me from the first minute we met. When the news media reported that Jerry had passed away, I was grief-stricken.

CHAPTER 24

Jacqueline and me were vacationing in Las Vegas with friends in 1997 when I saw that Frank Sinatra, Jr., was appearing at the Four Queens. We went to see him perform with his thirty-five piece band. His singing was great, his arrangements excellent, and he kept to the up-tempo tunes.

After the show I went to say hello to him and he remembered I was Sam Butera's road manager. I said, "You've progressed very well from when you started."

I wondered if he had forgotten his disastrous gig at the Holiday Inn thirty years earlier but I had the sense not to mention it. It didn't matter in the least now that he was singing great and had matured into his own style.

A few years later I was in the City in Little Italy for the San Genaro feast, the annual September street festival celebrating the patron saint of Naples that brings one million people to Mulberry Street and the surrounding neighborhood. Frank Junior was doing a show there sponsored by the Sorrento Cheese Company. He had his big band with Bill Miller as conductor, and thirty-plus musicians featuring lots of brass. I had met Bill Miller years earlier. I had sat in the sun that day since I had found a seat in an open-air grandstand. It had been hot, probably in the 90's.

Suddenly I spotted Angela Jennifer Lambert, who I knew as A.J. She's Nancy Sinatra's daughter and Frank Sinatra's granddaughter. I left my seat to greet her. I said, "I'm a friend of your grandfather."

"Where are you sitting?" she asked me.

"Up in the back."

"Come down here and sit with my guests and me."

She didn't take no for an answer and seated me next to Steve Tyrrell, who sang "The Way You Look Tonight" in the Steve Martin movie *Father of the Bride.*

The show started and it was fantastic. Frank Junior's voice was great and in perfect pitch. At the end of the show I went to say hello to

Frank Junior and Bill Miller. This time Frank Junior said he remembered me from the Westchester Premier Theater, when Sam did a song he recorded with his father and Bill conducted called "Stargazer." Bill was now 93 years old, but still very sharp. We reminisced about when we all had hung out at Jilly's.

Frank Junior laughed. "I remembered the long night with William B. Williams and the rest of my father's closest friends."

As I was about to say goodbye, A. J. asked me to join them for lunch at The Clam House. At first I declined the invitation but A.J. and Bill insisted I join them, so I did. I had a great time meeting old friends we had worked with at various shows. I said goodbye to all, and only a few days later, I read in the newspaper and saw on TV that Bill Miller had passed away. As sad as I was about Bill's death, I was happy that I'd been able to see him again and spend some time with him. What a great conductor he was!

Connie Stevens was going to do a show at the Claridge Hotel in Atlantic City for five nights. Her brother Chuck, as I have mentioned, was Sam Butera's drummer and my best friend. Before the gig he said to me, "Bobby, I would like it if you would be a bodyguard for my sister while she's in town."

"That's fine with me. In fact, it's more than fine."

"All you have to do is carry personal items from her room to the backstage area. You'll walk her back to her room after the show."

That night Chuck, his wife Kim, and Jacqueline were sitting up front watching the show while I guarded Connie Stevens' bag with my life. I didn't ask what was in it. I didn't care what was in it. I just kept that bag around my wrist. When the show ended, I met Connie backstage, and walked her to her suite.

"Here's your bag," I said as I handed it to her. "Have a good night."

She nodded. "Give my love to Jacqueline."

"You bet."

When closing night came, it was customary for the star of the show to throw a party. Some of the celebrities at Connie's were actor/comedian/impressionist John Byner, actress Shari Belafonte (Harry Belafonte's daughter), and the band members from the show.

CONNIE STEVENS AND ME

The following year Connie was back by popular demand to do her show again at the Claridge. This time her closing party was at the Portofino Restaurant on Pacific Avenue. I was sitting with Al Viola's son, who was Connie's drummer. Al Viola used to be Frank Sinatra's guitar player. Sitting with Connie were Don Costa's wife, (Don Costa had been an arranger for Mr. S.), Miles Davis's wife, and many other friends of Connie's from Long Port, a town near Atlantic City.

After a lot of picture-taking and the best Italian food ever, with the booze flowing all night long, the check came. The tab for the party was seven thousand dollars. At that point Connie called me over and asked me, "What do you think, Bobby, did everyone have a good time?"

"Connie the food was out of this world and the champagne flowed all night. You sure threw one hell of a party."

We hung out that night into the wee hours of the morning. Connie Stevens was very good to Jacqueline and me. We got together with her whenever we were in Las Vegas at the same time. Whenever Connie was in town to meet her brother Chuck, we visited with them. We were very close to both of them. When Jacqueline and me traveled to Vegas, Connie had us stay at her home, sometimes with Chuck and Kim.

One year Connie invited Jacqueline and me for Thanksgiving at her new home in Jackson Hole, Wyoming. That's the kind of person she was. Every time a group of us walked on the boardwalk in Atlantic City, Connie looked around and asked, "Where's Jacqueline?" She didn't walk away until Jacqueline came into sight. It was the same when we all walked from her suite to her show: Connie, Chuck, Kim, Jacqueline, and me. Connie stopped walking and looked for Jacqueline and didn't take another step until she saw her behind us.

One year she came into New York City from Los Angeles and wanted to visit her father's grave to pay her respects. I found out where her father was buried, and before Connie arrived I went to the gravesite to make sure everything had been kept up. After that I went to the gravesite from time to time and cleaned up the area. Connie's father was Teddy Stevens who had been a well-known jazz bass player in his own right, working at popular nightclubs and supper clubs.

After arriving in New York, Connie picked us up in her limo and we went to the cemetery with her, Kim, and Kim's two sons. We stopped at a flower shop, where she purchased three huge, beautiful flower arrangements for her Dad's grave. Connie placed the flowers on the grave and we all said our prayers and left. She never forgot her father and always paid her respects when she came to New York. She was the type who didn't forget her roots; she was the most caring person you ever wanted to meet. She has a genuine kindness that warms her lovely smile and casts her spiritual beauty.

Once we'd left the cemetery Connie suggested that we go to Brooklyn to see her old neighborhood. She was raised on Gates Avenue in the Bedford-Stuyvesant section and we drove past the house where she grew up. She reminisced about her childhood and asked to go and visit St. Barbara's Church she'd attended as a child. After we left the church, we all went for lunch at the Sage Diner and naturally, when the people in the diner recognized Connie, they came and asked for her autograph. The owner came over to greet her and her family.

When we left the diner, Connie asked me, "Is there a toy store around here?"

"There's one on Metropolitan Avenue, not far from where we are." As we entered the store, Connie told her nephews to pick out whatever they liked. The two kids, of course, got very excited and picked out the toys they wanted.

After that we all went to the Crown Plaza Hotel near LaGuardia Airport and the driver dropped us off. Connie kissed and hugged us all and drove off to the airport to catch her flight back to Los Angeles.

***

My daughter Lisa, Jacqueline, and me visited Las Vegas in 1998 and we went to see Hawaiian singer Don Ho perform at the Flamingo Hotel in Laughlin, Nevada. Don was a very dear friend of Sam's. I got to meet Don before his show and I mentioned, "I was Sam's road manager back east."

"Is that so? I love Sam. During my show I want you to come onstage and sing."

I sang "New York, New York." Did you know I can sing tolerably well before a forgiving audience when put on the spot. The crowd went wild. There must have been a lot of New Yorkers there. After the show my family and me took pictures with Don and he invited us to visit him in Hawaii.

When we were with Don in Hawaii, he confirmed the truth of a story the media had reported at one time that Elvis Presley wanted to do the Hawaiian wedding song and Don Ho had told him, "As long as you don't change the arrangement, you can do the song."

"Those were my exact words," he emphasized.

I've always said that Don Ho has the smoothest, softest voice you'd ever want to hear. I could listen to it endlessly without getting tired of it.

WITH DON HO

AND HIS BAND

Jacqueline came home from work one day and told me that her co-worker Connie Venieris had a couple of comp rooms in Atlantic City. She asked me if we could join the co-worker and her husband there the following week and have some fun. The first night in Atlantic City the four of us went to Harrah's and had a blast. The other couple slept in the following morning, but Jacqueline and me, both early risers, went down to have breakfast. As we were eating, I noticed singer Frankie Valli at the cashier paying for his breakfast. Frankie was known as the front man of the Four Seasons. I always liked to hear him sing "Sherry" and "Can't Take My Eyes Off of You." I got up and went over to speak to him. "Hello, I'm Bobby Lauri, Sam Butera's road manager." Before I could continue, fans started coming over to ask him for his autograph.

Frankie was a good friend of my best friend Chuck Stevens. Chuck had passed away a short time before this and I knew that, when you're busy on the road, you can't keep in touch with people.

When the autograph seekers had gone, I said to him, "Frankie, I don't know if you have heard that Chuck Stevens passed away not long ago."

Frankie Valli was startled. "All I heard," he said, "was that Chuck was sick. I'm so sorry to hear that news. Where are you sitting?"

"I'm sitting with my wife over there." I pointed to my table, where Jacqueline was waiting.

"Let me pay my bill," he said, "and I'll come over and talk." When he came over and sat down, I introduced him to Jacqueline and then started to tell him what had happened to Chuck.

"Chuck's wife Kim told me that we'd lost him. She said, 'We were home and Chuck didn't feel well. He had pain in both his arms. I called the ambulance and it came right away to take him to Humana Hospital, which was the closest to the house. But there was a championship fight in Vegas that night and traffic was jammed all over town, bumper to bumper. They couldn't even get down Las Vegas Boulevard. They finally got him to University Medical Center, where he passed away."

Jacqueline and I had been planning to fly out to Vegas the following week, but, of course, we flew out the next day. I loved Chuck more than any friend I ever had. He was more like a brother to me than a friend. I had never been one who listened to the opinions of other people or cared what they thought. But Chuck and me went out for coffee after each of Sam's shows and we talked about things going on with the band. If I said anything that was out of order, Chuck didn't hesitate to tell me so, and I loved him for that.

Chuck and me used to room together when we were on the road, and he's one of the few people I'd shared my hopes and dreams with. He did the same with me.

When you reach my age, you inevitably lose many of the people you've cared about in your life. Chuck Stevens and my brother-in-law Sally are the two people that I've missed the most since they passed away.

Knowing my story, you recognize that I can't say the same for my father Patsy. But I thank God with all my heart that He sent me other truly wonderful people with whom I have been able to share redeeming love.

I had been in the prime of my life. By the late 1970s I was a happy, successful man with a healthy, thriving young family and I'd come a long way in conquering the demons left over from my mostly loveless childhood and my father's abuse. By that time Patsy was a weak old man. He was dependent on others, which he absolutely hated. I only saw him because he lived in my boyhood home in Corona, where one of my sisters lived as well. So, my visits were really to her.

During one visit he asked me to bring him to the Italian Club by Spaghetti Park. We walked together up Corona Avenue from his house to the club. We had been walking quietly without conversation; and maybe it was being back in the old neighborhood with him and seeing him frail and dependent, which made me suddenly break the silence by saying, "You know, it's really funny how now that you are old and feeble I could choke the life out of you right here on this street corner without shedding a tear."

Patsy frowned. "You were a son-of-a–bitch growing up!"

"Look who made me that way. You still don't realize my behavior had a lot to do with the way you brought me up. You have no understanding that all the beatings I got from you had everything to do with it!"

It was the closest I'd ever come to telling him what I felt he'd done to my life. After that conversation he had nothing further to say to me. He was as unreachable and in as complete denial as ever.

Patsy died in 1981. I remember standing at his coffin, looking at him in it with pity. My brother-in-law Mike put his arm around my shoulder as I stood there trying to muster up a feeling of forgiveness for him. When I did feel something of that emotion, it was not for him, but for me. Sad to say, bitterness about my past has remained with me all my life.

I still wonder what Mike was thinking. Did he want to console me? That would be the joke of the year. Patsy died, my mother died, my sister Nancy died, her husband George died; and I didn't shed a single tear at any of their wakes. I eventually cried deeply for Nancy, who got a bad deal dying relatively young of cancer at the age of sixty-five. But other than for her, the only one I've cried for was my cat Sam.

Sam got hit by a car and I found him dead in the street. I picked him up and brought him back to my house. I started to bury him and couldn't do it. I was crying so much for that cat that my son Michael had to bury him. He couldn't bear to leave me there with him, as he saw how miserable I was. That cat showed me more love by far in his three years than Patsy did in my whole lifetime. It's sad to think how, as a child, I did not have one happy day living in his household. Patsy Lauri, you were one angry man and you made everyone around you fear for their lives!

CHAPTER 25

After twenty years in the temperature-control business in New York, I applied for a position as a thermostat repairer for the New York City Police Department. As I filled out the application, I came to the question, "Have you ever been arrested?" I was stuck. If I put down that I had been arrested many years earlier, I might not be approved for the position. So before I completed and sent in my application by mail, I made a trip to the Queens County Courthouse.

One of the court officers there directed me to a room where all the arrest records going back many years were filed. He told me to ask the clerk there to find my 1965 file. The clerk checked her computer first, but the computer system was relatively new and she found nothing. I gave her my full name and the year of the incident, but she still found nothing. Then, she looked through all of her microfiche records and still came up with nothing. I said to the clerk, "There must be something here, some kind of record that shows when I was arrested."

"Look sir," she said. "I have nothing here. Your name doesn't come up anywhere, so according to my records there was no arrest."

I was very persistent, wanting to be absolutely sure that I was leaving no stone unturned under which something might come back to bite me if I went to work for the city.

The clerk said, "Look, there's a room behind my office and in that room you will find shelves and shelves full of books of arrests. If you want to go take a look to ease your mind, the room is yours."

"Okay, I'll do it."

Then, she said, "You know, in this computer age that's coming everything will be in the computer and there will be no more writing in books: no names, no arrest dates, no charges filed. And I'll tell you something else—those books back there are going to be shredded soon, so this could be your last chance to look at them."

I went into the back room and started looking through book after book after book. I must have gone through about fifteen books and was about ready to give up. Then I saw one more book dated 1965. I opened it up and turned page after page. I spotted my name! Thank God, the charges against me had all been dropped.

I went to the front of the courthouse to complete and submit the police-department application and where it said, "Have you ever been arrested?" I wrote, "Yes, but never convicted of any crime or felony." I continued through the entire application process, which included a full detailing of my history.

Three months later I was informed that I'd been invited to a New York City Police Department job interview. The interview went well, and I was hired right away. I was very proud of the job I got, in the Building Maintenance Section (BMS). After six years I was transferred to police headquarters, where I did my remaining time until I retired on August 25, 2002.

At 4:30 a.m. on the morning of September 11, 2001 I left home just as I always did to reach my job at NYPD headquarters at 1 Police Plaza by 5:00 a.m. Parking was at a premium downtown and if you didn't get in by that hour, two hours before sign-in, you were stuck with your car without a parking spot. You'd have to park all the way down by the East River and, boy, what a walk that was. If you got a parking spot in the rows of spots available for employees, you had to set a wristwatch alarm for 7:30 a.m. (0730 in military-time of the Police Department). Then you'd sleep in your car until you awoke. At that time, you'd hear alarms starting to go off down the rows of cars where we all took our naps before signing in for work.

The sun was shining brightly as I made my way to my work place on the fifteenth floor of police headquarters. I was having my morning coffee at around 8:30 a.m. with the chief engineers when all of a sudden we heard a bang that sounded unusually loud. We all looked at each other with the sense that something very much out of the ordinary had happened.

Then this guy Kyle and me took the stairs to the roof. We thought it might've been an electrical motor that exploded. When we found that wasn't the case, we walked up another staircase to check the water tanks, but the floor was totally dry, so that couldn't have been it either. We were about to head back down to finish our coffee, when I said to Kyle, "It's a beautiful day. While we're up here, let's take a walk up to the heliport."

The NYPD heliport was only one more flight up from where we had been. Just then sirens began to wail all around us and as we reached the heliport, we saw that the North Tower of the World Trade Center nearby was smoking like it was on fire.

Looking at the heavily smoking tower, I said to Kyle, "A small plane must have hit the World Trade Center."

It was indeed a plane, but not a small one. And there was a fire, which seemed localized despite much billowing smoke. We stood there watching and from where Kyle stood he didn't see a second plane coming around the west side of Tower A, which was the South Tower. Suddenly, I saw what looked like a black airliner heading toward the tower. It was actually the shadow behind the sun that made the plane look black.

I screamed, "Look, Kyle!" The plane was coming in low, heading directly into the South Tower.

Kyle shouted, "I can't believe what I'm seeing!"

We were both frightened, but I didn't say a word. I just stood there in shock.

People on the street heard and saw that plane crash into the building. From where Kyle and me stood, way above the streets at the heliport, we saw the whole plane go right into the South Tower at around the 86th-story level. That plane didn't just crash into the building, it disappeared into it. I realized then that it was some kind of terror attack against our country and feared that police headquarters would be next.

I took the elevator down to street level and headed toward Chinatown. I saw a pay phone and decided to call my sister Susan. It was a miracle that the phone worked, and it was another miracle that Susan answered, as she often did not. When she picked up the phone, I said to her, "Did you hear from Hannah?"

Hannah was my niece and she worked in the South Tower for a big investment banking company.

"No," Susan said. "I haven't spoken to anyone yet and she hasn't called us either."

"I guess you know by now," I said to Susan, "that we are under attack and that two planes just went into the World Trade Center towers. I gotta go now."

Fearing for my life, I hung up the phone, and started to run with many other people away from the dense cloud of soot that began to envelop everything. Where everyone was running I couldn't tell. It felt like it was the end of the world! Everyone was frightened to death!

People handle emotions differently when in shock. Some people have a drink; some people smoke cigarettes or a joint. I found myself feeling as if I had a great need to eat. It was at that moment that I realized I was an emotional eater. I stopped in a Chinese bakery and had a cup of coffee and a piece of cake. Some people may think that was the worst time to eat and drink, and I wouldn't really blame them. But I wasn't eating or drinking out of enjoyment; I was eating and drinking as a way of trying to calm down from the powerful emotions I had just experienced.

Then the second tower collapsed. I wasn't conscious of the first tower's fate– and the soot and debris covered all of downtown.

Dazed I made my way back to police headquarters. I was trying to enter the building when an officer said, "Go home. We're not letting anyone back in the building."

I raced to my car and found about eight inches of ash over the car: on the roof, the windshield, the hood, and the rear window. I used my hands to clean off the car enough to see out of the front and side windows. The Williamsburg Bridge was closed, so I decided to take Third Avenue uptown. I drove from downtown all the way up to 125th Street and over the Triborough Bridge. It seemed like every car in Manhattan was trying to reach the bridge and it took me three and a half hours to do so. The

Triborough Bridge and Tunnel Authority had lifted tolls that day and waved every car through without paying.

During the drive that seemed to last forever I thought back to when I saw the plane hit the South Tower, remembering that my niece Hannah worked on an upper floor. I didn't know the exact floor, but I knew it was above where the plane had hit. I hoped she'd made it out of the building.

Later that night when I'd finally made it home, I found out that nobody had heard from her, and my heart just sank. Hannah died in the terror attack that day. She had grown up in a very large family and she had a personality you couldn't help but love. She always had a smile on her face and also had a good word for everyone. She was always up, never down. I'd had conversations with her about family problems, issues I'd had with family members, and if I asked her opinion, she always put a lid on whatever had me steaming. She had a way of calming down family tensions. She had a very kind heart and she loved everybody. She was known for giving away possessions, such as her vacuum cleaner, her iron, and other items people needed.

The next day I walked the short distance from headquarters to the site with Officer Rodriguez who I worked with. The devastation was mind-boggling. Cement, glass, wood, and metal were piled about 200 feet high, with girders of steel sticking out like giant spikes. The National Guard was at the site keeping people back a safe distance.

As weeks went by, the Police and Fire Departments and construction workers pulled body after body out of heaps of rubble. When my son-in-law Tom, who works for the New York City Fire Department, had pulled up to the site in his fire truck just before the buildings came down, he was approached by an FDNY captain frantically waving his arms to tell him to back his rig up. If that captain hadn't been there, Tom and his fellow firefighters in the rig most likely would have been crushed to death. As the buildings came down, the debris covered blocks and blocks of the surrounding area. There was no safe hiding place. If you didn't run fast enough to get out of the way, you were a goner.

People came to the site every day, including me and other NYPD personnel, volunteering to do anything we could to help, even if it was just giving out bottled water to the many emergency workers. Eventually, the National Guard started to keep everybody away because they knew that better-organized long-term help from the Red Cross and other charity organizations was being coordinated. St. Paul's Church on Broadway sent the largest contingent of volunteers for the work. God bless those people who gave of themselves for months and months at a time! God bless all the firefighters and the police for risking their lives at that place!

The Friday after the attack Detective John Perry, who had been set to retire that very day, decided to go to the pile to help with moving the debris and rescuing people. Earlier that day before John had decided to go there, I had been by his office with a crew of men cleaning out the ceiling vents. We had gone from floor to floor to do this, because the vents on all the floors were clogged with the heavy, choking dust from the collapse of the Twin Towers. I congratulated John on his retirement and then I asked him for the keys to his office so we could continue to clean his vents up to 11 p. m. We had starting this work at 3 p. m. At first he was reluctant to give me the keys because there were a lot of private files in his office, but I reassured him that first thing Monday morning I would personally come to his office and return his keys.

I was there by 8 a.m. that Monday and I went to John's office, opened the door, and then waited for quite a while until a fellow officer approached me and asked, "Did you hear about John Perry?"

"No, I haven't heard."

"Last Friday on John Perry's last day of work he went to "Ground Zero" to see if he could be of any help. He died there."

"God rest his soul in peace." My stomach fell just like those buildings. I felt miserable. John had been such a likable man and a fine police officer. He worked heart and soul for the Department.

For the rest of that week I went to work the same way I had done for years. I took the Williamsburg Bridge, made a left turn on Allen Street, and made a right on Henry Street to headquarters. Before the attack I used to admire the view of the beautiful towers as I drove down Henry Street, with all of their windows glowing in the morning light. After the towers fell, I drove down Henry Street with a horrible feeling in the pit of my stomach. There was nothing to look at no more, no towers, no windows, and no lights, just the sky. It was an empty sight, and day after day all I smelled was the smell of the corpses of those poor people who had gone to work faithfully day after day to support their families. The smell lingered for a long, long time.

Counseling in the auditorium at headquarters was offered to us. I went that week but it didn't help me feel any better. One day I got a call from one of the engineers at police headquarters. He said to me, "Bobby, you have to do something about the smell coming into the building through the Heating, Ventilation, and Air-Conditioning (HVAC). People are calling down to my office from various floors and telling me the odor was getting them sick and that they have to leave the building and go home."

"If I close all the outside air dampers it would overheat the building."

"You've got to do something," he insisted.

So I closed down the outside dampers and that sort of helped, but not enough to remove all of the smell. Every day from September through December we endured the stench of death. When December 31st came around, I put in my retirement papers. First, I went on terminal leave, and then took all my vacation time, which supported me up until August 25th, 2002. I went on full retirement at age sixty-one and have never looked back. I wasn't able to bring myself to go down to Ground Zero until 2004, when I went to see my niece Hannah's name on the posters. Now her name is engraved on a permanent wall.

CHAPTER 26

After experiencing the devastation of the 9/11 terror attacks so closely, I jumped at Sam Butera's invitation to go to Florida to join him and The Wildest on tour and have some fun. After every show we went straight back to our hotel because we had to get back in the van the next morning, right after breakfast, and travel to our next venue. This was a ten-day tour starting out in Coral Springs, on to Melbourne, then to Daytona Beach, all on Florida's east coast. Then we crossed the state and went west to Sarasota, Clearwater, Fort Myers, and then back across the state on Route 75 to the final gig at Boca Raton.

We were back in the van every morning. It was the roughest road trip with Sam I ever had. I didn't even unpack my suitcase. Every night I left the clothes I was going to wear the next day on top of the inside of the suitcase.

The following year Sam called me again. "Bobby, how about joining me for a two-week gig in Florida? I'm touring with Julius La Rosa." Some of Julius' hits were *"Domani," "Eh, Compare,"* "Anywhere I Wander," and many other great songs.

I told Sam, "The last trip had really tired me out."

"This trip will be different with Julie," Sam said. "We'll be staying one hotel and every night will drive to a new venue. Then we'll come back to the hotel where we're staying."

"That sounds good. I'll come."

On tour with us were the Gaylords, whose hits were "The Little Shoemaker," "From the Vine Came the Grapes," and many more great songs.

The gigs were fun. We were seven in the van: Sam in the front seat with our driver Nick Boccuzi, Julie La Rosa in the middle next to Burt Holiday and Ron Gaylord, in the back bass player Hank Mills next to me.

ME AND THE GAYLORDS

Another night at 1:00 a.m. we were eating at an Italian restaurant with some friends. I ordered something light and Sam ordered his favorite dish, eggplant *parmigiana*, which he always ordered. Julius La Rosa ordered sausage, meatballs, and peppers in a red sauce. I asked him, "Julie, are you going to eat that at this late hour?"

"Why not? It's okay."

"If I ate that at this hour," I said, "they'd be pumping my stomach at the hospital."

He just laughed and enjoyed his meal. I was jealous. Sam started to laugh also. The rest of the road trip went fine, and we all had a blast.

Sam asked me to do another tour in Florida from February 21st through March 2nd, 2003. We did different condo shows in many condo developments, such as Venetian Isles; Hemispheres; Kings Point Tamarac; the Township in Coconut Creek; and the Century Villages of Boca Raton, Deerfield Beach, Pembroke Pines, and West Palm Beach.

JULIUS LA ROSA AND ME

One morning, while me and my friend Mikey Pennachio were having breakfast in the hotel, Sam came down to join us. He told me that he was going to Las Vegas for a thirteen-day layover and he wanted me to drive with him to Los Angeles to do the House of Blues Jazz Club. He told me he had booked a room for me at the Palace Station Casino in Las Vegas.

"I don't want to be by myself for thirteen days in Las Vegas. I'll go back east and meet you in April in Atlantic City to do the "Sands' Nostalgia Shows of the Year."

Sam was on the bill with The Trainers' and Freddy Bell.

ME AND FREDDIE BELL

I met Sam in April and we did the show. It brought in a tremendous number of fans from New York, New Jersey, South Philly, and elsewhere in Pennsylvania. The shows were sold out every night. That was the last time I was to go on tour with Sam.

Freddie Bell was well known in his entertainment career in Atlantic City and Las Vegas. He was one of the great lounge show performers of that era. He was a great guy and a good friend and I spent many nights in the AC and LV with him.

Sam was booked at Westbury Music Fair in 2004 for a show featuring Sam Butera and the Wildest and Al Martino. I was at the venue that night doing the sound check with the stagehands when I noticed I had not seen Sam arrive yet. I asked one of the theater staff if he knew where Sam was and when he didn't answer, I went outside and called Sam's home number. To my surprise Sam answered the phone.

"Sam," I asked. What happened? You forgot you had a gig at The Music Fair?"

"Bobby, I didn't want to tell you I wasn't going to make that job. My mind wanted to come, but my feet can't move."

The rest of the band did the show and they were great. Al Martino sang his heart out.

That January Sam went to the hospital. He never recovered and lingered in a weakened state for five years. Sam passed away in June of 2009. I became so sick to my stomach when I learned of his death that I couldn't bring myself to go to his funeral. I'd been with Sam as a friend and confidant since 1969. I had the best times of my life with that man. "God bless you in Heaven, Sam! Always remember what Louie Prima use to say, 'Play pretty for the people.' We're listening to you as you play with the angels."

I'll never forget how Sam ended every show with "When the Saints Go Marching In" and then he addressed the audience, "Remember, it's nice to be important, but it's important to be nice. Thank you for being so nice to us. Have a great evening!"

GOOD BYE TO MY DEAR FRIEND SAM BUTERA

Made in the USA
Columbia, SC
19 June 2023

17959465R00114